SONIA JOHNSON
WILDFIRE
IGNITING THE SHE/VOLUTION

SONIA JOHNSON
WILDFIRE
IGNITING THE SHE/VOLUTION

WILDFIRE BOOKS

Albuquerque, New Mexico 87184

Inquiries about speaking engagements, workshops, and tapes of speeches should be directed to Susan Horwitz, P. O. Box 10286, Albuquerque, NM 87184, (505) 344-4790.

Inquiries should be addressed to:
Wildfire Books, P.O. Box 10598, Albuquerque, NM 87184 (505) 344-6499

Cover art and design: Diana Souza

Cover photograph: Charlene Eldridge Wheeler

Printed in the United States of America

Library of Congress Cataloging-in-Publication Data

Johnson, Sonia.
    Wildfire : igniting the she/volution / Sonia Johnson.
        p.   cm.
    Includes index.
    ISBN 1-87761-700-8. $10.95
        2. Women's rights—United States.   2. Patriarchy—United States.
    3. Feminism—United States.   4. Control (Psychology)   I. Title.
    HQ1236.5.U6S65   1989
    305.42'0973—dc20   89-9076
                                                                        CIP

ISBN 1-877617-00-8

With Love and Thanks

to Christine Champion for her courage in becoming my publishing partner in the daring enterprise, Wildfire Books. Also for opening her home and her hand to me during the last three months of the writing of this book. Her friendship is a constant blessing in my life;

to Susan Horwitz for co-conspiring with me, for coming up with the right ideas at the right times, and for turning her experience and skill to the actual publishing of this book. She works with me on the level of magic;

to Genevieve Vaughan for her understanding of gift giving. She has changed deeply and forever the way I perceive the world;

to Marlene Mountain, poet from Hampton, Tennessee, from whose deliciously unconventional brain Susan picked the word "She/Volution" for the subtitle. Also for the others of her lexic creations that liven up the text;

to Diana Souza for her dream-level communication with me that inspired a cover design as passionate and wild as my vision;

to my son Marc for his patience with my many frantic phone calls and for his expert guidance through the mazes of the WordPerfect word processing program;

to Adele Gorelick and Janet Mullaney for editing this book under wildly fluctuating publishing circumstances, and to Pat McBride and Lorna Gold Marchand for helping with the onerous job of proofreading;

to Susan Britt of the English Department at the University of New Mexico in Albuquerque for the organizational insight that helped me write a completely different Part III;

and to Mary Daly, whose thinking cracked my conditioning open years ago and keeps it open, for her unwavering dedication to women. Also for her brilliant contributions to our language—concepts such as "biophilic," "fembot," and "patriarchal reversal" for instance—that are now integral to feminist discourse.

For Kari, daughter and friend,
whose wild creative fire is a beacon to me

Contents

Preface

T his is a self-published book. Late in its writing I
realized that it could not be otherwise because it is a
book about how to get free. In it I present as strong an
argument as I can for women not only to disengage
psychically and emotionally from patriarchy and all its
institutions but to detach materially and economically as
well. The guiding principle of my life, "the means are the
ends," has taught me that our participation in a corrupt
system facilitates it and corrupts and therefore defeats us.

The implications of this permeate my life. They mean,
for instance, that I must make the bravest possible day-
by-day effort to live the theory I write if my work is to be
useful in women's current global task of liberating first
our own and consequently the human mind.

What this belief dictates to me, for example, is that if
it is true that the means are the ends, then since I want a
world in which women do not have to compromise in
order to survive, I cannot compromise now. Also, if I
want a world in which women are in control of their lives,
I must be in control of my own life as fully as possible

now. In addition, since I want a world in which artists are neither abused nor exploited, I must remove myself from as many such eventualities as I can right now. And since I long for a world in which women are not ruled by our fear of economic deprivation, right now I must stop being afraid.

Knowing, therefore, that only out of my own personal integrity could my work have integrity and power, I retrieved this and my first book, *From Housewife to Heretic,* from their publishers and determined from this time forth to publish my own work.

Taking on this task[1] means in part that I have had to look closely and seriously at patriarchal publishing conventions. As I have, I have realized that I must still bow to some of them—selling books for money, for instance, trying if possible to make a profit.[2]

But there is one convention that I think needs to be discarded immediately, and that is the practice of enlisting well-known or famous people to write words of endorsement and praise for the cover. As a feminist dedicated to a new, nonhierarchical paradigm and trying therefore in as many ways as I can in my own life to stop perpetuating the "star" system, I have had to dare to let my picture and a quote bear the entire burden of representing this book to

---

[1] Side by side with two wonderfully strong and competent friends, Christine Champion and Susan Horwitz.

[2] I say this though I expect in my lifetime to see money and barter disappear, as the basic patriarchal belief that exchange is an economic given dies an inevitable death.

the prospective buyer. If *Wildfire* speaks to the hearts of many and diverse women, as I hope it will, it must speak entirely for itself.

Knowing that my work cannot be disconnected from my life, and considering my life an experiment, it is in the spirit of experiment that I offer this record of my thinking and changing. My daily privilege of living as a feminist is for me the most compelling exploration of myself, offering me chance after chance to care more deeply, to dare more audaciously, every moment full of new, almost unthinkable, possibilities for being, invitations to live boldly.

Though I write with the authority of having traveled much of the road I describe and am passionate and sure, I do not mean to be either dogmatic or prescriptive. I recognize that women are not clones, that we are going to disagree to some extent for a very long time about what needs to be done and how. I write *Wildfire* more to ease and please my own heart, to clarify for myself who and why I am.

I also write to remain quietly present to myself, my spirit pliable, my psyche malleable, as my witch/goddess Self molds me into the woman I must be to step out of this wreck of a system; to step out onto the radiant plain of female ways and times where the great fires of women's creativity blaze from horizon to horizon against the night sky, burning away the dross, purifying, bursting the seed pods—at once planting and harvesting.

WILDFIRE

Kindled by the flames of women's untamable creative powers, I enchant, I see visions, I prophesy.
I prepare to make miracles.

Albuquerque, New Mexico
January 1989

Part I

UP OFF OUR KNEES

Preface to Part I

In November 1987, when *Going Out of Our Minds: The Metaphysics of Liberation* was due for its third printing, I eagerly reworked Chapter 13 before it went again to press. I had come to believe that the reason Chapter 13 was the most misunderstood portion of the book was because the concepts in that chapter had been the least clear to me as I wrote.

But I had recently completed a three-month, thirty-city book tour that had included at least fifty speeches and a tremendous amount of talking about my theory of change—personal and planetary. So much excellent on-the-spot thinking had compelled me to understand better, to expand, to make new connections, and to find more comprehensible ways to explain the phenomena I was describing and the activism I was advocating. So as I began to rewrite, I was reeling with excitement at the new possibilities that were opening up in my mind.

But in the middle of it somewhere I became aware of the by-now-familiar feeling that something was out of tune. As I searched inside myself for whatever it was that was not in harmony, I found the discordant note almost at once.

In the Preface of *Going Out of Our Minds*, I introduced the idea of "process theory"—theory that reveals not only the thinker's conclusions but also the journey by which she arrived at them. The case for process theory is based on the assumption that the journey is as valuable as the destination and that they cannot be disconnected without diminishing both; but more than that, that the journey *is* the destination.

I realized that because Chapter 13 truly represented the stage of thinking I had reached at the time of its publication, it must stand as it was. If I had anything else to say, to honor my own development I needed to begin a new record that demonstrated the continuity and dynamism of both theory and process. I needed to be certain not to seem to be repudiating either of them by revising.

So *Wildfire* opens with the material I originally wrote to replace Chapter 13 but that was never published in *Going Out of Our Minds*. Though Chapters 1 and 2 refine the theory I outlined in the former book, they do not begin where *Going Out of Our Minds* ends. Instead, they overlap it, in a couple of instances looking at the same material from other perspectives.

Chapter 3, the logical extension of Chapters 1 and 2, is completely new material. The basic idea of it came to me one night during the Q and A session after my speech as I was trying urgently to clarify my point of view. As I grasped the idea and began to use it, light broke over the faces of the audience, brows unfurrowed, and heads nodded. I knew from the response that I had stumbled upon something important and probably true, something that would advance our understanding of how women are first brought to our knees, then how we are kept there, and finally how we can stand up straight again and walk away free.

CHAPTER 1

Who's Afraid of the Supreme Court?

After one of my workshops at the Michigan Women's Music Festival in the summer of 1987, a woman came up to talk to me. She told me she had been working frantically day and night for the preceding two months to keep Bork off the Supreme Court. She had been writing letters and organizing others to write, holding public meetings, distributing flyers, talking to the media, setting up telephone networks—desperately doing everything she could think of. Her panic drove her into insomnia and depression and began to affect her health.

So she had come to Michigan to try to relax and rest but until my workshop had not been able to do so. As she listened to me, however, she thought, "What if she's right? What if it really doesn't matter who's on the Supreme Court?" Immediately, she felt as if an enormous burden had fallen from her shoulders. Her body felt light

7

and buoyant, full of energy and zest. Feeling as if she hadn't breathed for two months, she filled her lungs with clear rain-washed air. The world that had appeared a uniform gray for so many weeks now glowed richly with color. She felt peaceful and happy—and this worried her.

"Do you think I'm just being *irresponsible*?" she asked nervously.

I know there are feminists who would have answered without hesitation, "Yes, I think you are!" But it seemed obvious to me that this woman, by daring to open herself to a seemingly fantastic possibility, had slipped through a crack in her programming and lived for a few precious moments in a free, nonpatriarchal world. I understood that for as long as she could stay outside her old beliefs and remain in the feeling of freedom she would be engaged in the actual creation of that new world. I told her I found her behavior eminently responsible, perhaps the only responsible behavior possible for women at this time in history.

It seems to me that to understand this, much depends on how we view the nature of reality. One of the most insistent messages from my inner voice in the last few years reaffirms the feminist revelation that among the myriad hoaxes of men, the biggest and most basic is what we are socialized to perceive as real. Since every second of my life is focused upon transforming "reality," I have had to think long and hard about that lie.

As I have asked myself: how does reality come into being? Why does it persist or die? I have known, of course, that there have always been voices among us insisting that what we perceive as reality has no objective existence. Though I have found this interesting, I didn't understand how it translated into daily life until I came across the following story.[1]

Several hundred years ago, Magellan and his men sailed into a harbor in the Tierra del Fuego islands in their tall ships, put down their anchors, and rowed ashore in rowboats. A few days later, the shaman called the islanders together and she[2] said, "I'm going to tell you something preposterous, so get ready. Those men couldn't have come across all that open sea in the little boats they landed on our beach in. That means—and this is the preposterous part—that there have to be big, *big* boats out there in the harbor." Everyone turned to look—and got goose bumps; all they could see was the shimmering blue water. "Really?" they asked. "Really," she answered.

Because I am tired of using examples about men from men's books, I occasionally ask women in my audiences to give me another example of this phenomenon, one with women as its main characters. Here is a Lesbian story with the same theme:

Heather and Ruth (not their real names) had lived together as lovers for many years in an otherwise straight neighborhood. Because of their jobs, they had chosen to remain deeply closeted. Even those neighbors with whom

---

[1] Lawrence Blair, *Rhythms of Vision: The Changing Patterns of Belief.* Schocken Books: New York, 1975, p. 22.

[2] This is the only change I've made in the story, but the men changed it first; I am merely restoring authenticity.

9

they were close believed they were merely house-mates.

For their bang-up fifteenth anniversary celebration, Heather hung a huge sign *in lights* above the front door, a sign so big and dazzling that it nearly bowled the arriving guests over: "Ruth darling, 15 wonderful years together! I love you. Heather."

Heather and Ruth's property was surrounded by a fence that blocked a view of the shining love letter from the street and from their neighbors' places. But that night, their married friend from next door, not realizing they were having guests over, decided to come around for a chat. She walked up the path to the front door, knocked, and found herself in the midst of a party. It soon became apparent that she wasn't just pretending out of embarrassment, she really did not even *suspect* the reason for the celebration. The woman who told me the story assured me that it was fact that the neighbor had looked directly at the blazing sign for 50 yards as she came up the walk, had stood ringing the doorbell directly beneath it, and *hadn't seen it at all.*

Of course we ask how the Tierra del Fuegans could *not* see the ships, with their tiers of white sails sparkling in the sun, billowing in the wind? How could Heather and Ruth's neighbor *not* see their sign? The ships, the sign—they were so obvious, so "real."

But they were not real to those who had no place for them in their world view. They could not see them because reality is what people *expect* to see in the harbor or on the front of their neighbor's house. Reality is what we *believe* we will see when we look there, what we think is possible, what we have been told to believe is true, very strong, inevitable, unchangeable, irrevocable. Reality is what we are conditioned to value, and therefore *what we pay attention to*. Reality is what we are taught to think god plunked down in front of us and we have no choice but to learn to live with the best we can. It is what is called "natural."

Reality, then, is an internal construct, and it is defined and controlled by the dominant group.[3] The moment we internalize men's propaganda, their reality comes to live in our hearts and minds. Then, projecting it out onto our external screen, out onto the harbor or our friend's front door, we proceed to interact with it in ways that make it concrete, that institutionalize it, that real-ize it. In order for it to continue, all of us have to wake up every morning and project again what we believe is real out onto our external screen and immediately begin again to connect with it in reciprocal ways. This is how we are intimately and every moment involved in its creation and perpetuation.

The implications of this are that by interacting with a totally different world right now, we can bring *it* into focus. Women's world never left this planet. It is still here, right in front of our noses. We recreate it as we learn to see it and to live in it.

---

[3] Andra Medea, "Medea's Laws of Conflict," from the text of a speech given at the 1987 annual Chimera conference and teacher training in Chicago, p. 9. This material is the basis of a forthcoming book tentatively titled *The Corporate Chimera*.

Though a basic lie of patriarchy is that "reality" is outside us, that it is someone else's creation and that therefore someone else has to change it, my hunch is that we, along with every living thing in the universe (and all is alive), are the creators of the world and that we daily recreate it from the stuff of our expectations and beliefs, from what we perceive as possible.

The question of the existence of "objectivity" is now before the worldwide scientific community. I have been much entertained by the uproar. For several hundred years now science has been almost synonymous with the Newtonian/Cartesian model of the world as machine—an object external and independent of us, ticking along like a great clock. The job of science has been to discover, describe, and use to advantage the laws by which the clock operates—laws, it has been assumed, that are entirely unaffected by human desire.

Now, of course, some scientists out on the fringes of credibility (but perhaps less and less so) are recognizing that results of experiments thought to be free of investigator bias are, in fact, *dictated* by that bias. That what develops in a petri dish, for instance, does not reveal the laws that govern the substances therein so much as it reveals the investigator's expectations and beliefs about what must inevitably develop there under certain conditions. In short, scientists are whispering with wide eyes that objectivity doesn't seem to be possible.

Sitting on a plane reading this, I smiled and murmured under my breath, "No kidding!" Women, who have always been belittled for our lack of "objectivity," have known in some deep, intuitive, and conclusive way that objectivity was a figment of men's fevered necessity to be in all things "not women," a phantom spawned by their panic to find their own male and superior ways of verifying truth, a way of being in control.

If the genesis of all reality is internal and subjective, all systems are internal systems, including patriarchy. Patriarchy does not then have a separate existence outside us; it exists inside us and we project it daily onto our external screen, onto our harbor the world, and then interact with it in ways that keep it functioning as we are taught to believe it must inevitably function.

The wonderfully hopeful part of this is that reality's being within us obviously makes it very much under our control. So much under our control, in fact, that the instant patriarchy dies in our hearts and in our minds, it dies everywhere. When women cease to believe that patriarchy is very strong, when we stop being afraid of it, when we stop believing that we must do everything through and in relation to men and their system, when we stop thinking of men's control as power, when we deprogram ourselves from the belief that we cannot build a new world without first getting men's approval (trying to get them to legislate it for us, for instance), and when we stop believing that we have to do any piece of our lives as society dictates, then patriarchy is over. The instant enough of us detach from patriarchy and stop facilitating it, that is the instant tyranny will cease.

We are learning how to look, how to see. We are not on our way to a new world, we are there already and must simply recognize it. Though we began by seeing our oppression, now we must see beyond it, see that our freedom is as real as our bondage, and that we can—and often do—live in it right now.

Once, to a group of friends, I talked about how, with my current understanding of my role in perpetuating patriarchy and because of my love for myself and women and all life, I had to let go, to detach, to cut the umbilical cords of belief and feeling. To illustrate what I meant, at least in part, I quoted my friend Sheila Feiger:

> I'm not interested in doing less than changing the world. But I've been in the movement—in NOW—for 12 years. I've carried the picket signs and gone to the conferences, been in the demonstrations, and spoken, and written letters, and watched Congress, and worked for candidates, and done all the things we thought would change the world. And I know that that is not the way to change the world and I'm not going to do those things anymore.

"And neither am I," I said to my friends.

"Oh, Sonia," one of them sighed, "that's just not practical!"

"Practical," I repeated thoughtfully. "Isn't that an interesting word." I thought to myself how for 5,000 years women have been resisting patriarchy in all the ways that have been called practical, resistance itself held to be the only practical avenue to change. Some say that women weren't always aware enough to resist or didn't know anything was wrong. But I say that if we want to

14

know how women were down through the centuries, all we have to do is look at ourselves. *We* are how women have been: brilliant, brave, strong—magnificent. All through history women have known, intuitively when not cerebrally, that patriarchy was deadly to everything we loved, and we have *always* resisted it in every way, overt and covert, private and public, that presented itself—the most creative, inventive, imaginative ways possible (and there are countless ways to resist, as we know) on all its levels. Women have resisted patriarchy with unsurpassed cunning, craft, and passion for at least 5,000 years.

I don't want to be hasty, but it seems to me that 5,000 years is long enough to try any method, particularly one that doesn't work. Women want above all else to be fair, and we have given resistance a fair trial. In all fairness then, it is time to try something different.

It should have been obvious to us, and would have been if we hadn't been so deeply conditioned to believe otherwise, that resistance *doesn't* work. When we look at the world, what we see is patriarchy at its nadir, in its decadence, patriarchy most fully itself, so ripe it is rotten. I think this is not *despite* women's resistance but *because* of it. There are women who want to believe that if we had not resisted, patriarchy would be even worse, that our resistance has been a sort of holding action. But nothing can be put on "hold"; all is constantly changing, as patriarchy grown obscenely, putrescently patriarchal, attests.

Then these women say, "My life is so much easier because of the women who fought before me. How can

I not do the same for my sisters?" But men give starving women crumbs to distract us from their escalating violence. They point out how they have improved women's lot. How women can now get men's jobs, can now attend the universities. What they are saying is that they have seen to it that we have a larger stake in their system. It is called co-optation.

What if the women who went before us had, instead of fighting against patriarchy, made a different world? If they had, the heritage they would have left us would be *no patriarchy at all*. That's the heritage I'm interested in leaving behind. More than that, that's what I want for myself right now.

From the field of Neuro-Linguistic Programming comes a useful rule for resisters: "if you always do what you've always done, you'll always get what you've always got. So if you want change, do *anything* else!"[4]

As I thought about resistance being the most powerful, albeit the most subtle, form of collaboration possible, and speculated about the mechanics of it, into my mind sprang a picture of a fortress on a hill—patriarchy!—with its pennants flying, its great bulwarks, its massive gate, and all the men ranged behind its walls being male-ly supreme.

Looking down the hill a short distance, I saw the women, thousands of them, a huge battering ram in their arms, crying "We've got to get through to the men!

---

[4] Correspondence from Rain On The Earth, Clearlake, CA, January 6, 1988; also letter from Kate Martin, St. Louis, Mo, January 15, 1988.

We've got to make them stop! We've got to get them to understand that they're destroying everything!" They run at the gate with the ram: Whoom! And again: Whoom! Over and over again, for five long millennia: Whoom! Whoom! Whoom! Some women are pole-vaulting over the walls, shouting as they leap: "If we can just get in there, we can change everything!" Through the centuries, women fall by the way but others quickly take their places and the desperate siege goes on, Whoom! Whoom!

With my mind's eye, I looked to see what was happening *behind* the gate during all this and I could see it as clearly as if I were actually there: the men, drunk with adrenalin, are being spurred by the assault to incredible heights of creativity. They have invented bionic metals to reinforce the gate and walls wherever the ram reveals a weak spot, gradually making the fortress impregnable, impenetrable—ah, the sexual terms we have in English for not being able to get through! The assault, by forcing them to strengthen, refine, and embellish the original edifice, serves to entrench patriarchy further with every Whoom!

I should have learned from this image—and from my experience of being a woman in patriarchy—what Susan Horwitz called to my attention about this scenario. "It's obvious," she said, "that resistance is an acknowledgment and an acceptance of powerlessness. And if we perceive ourselves as powerless, presto, we *are* powerless."

Motherhood should have taught me that resistance only causes deeper entrenchment. Any woman who has

17

had teenagers will testify that when kids are doing something they shouldn't be doing and Mother nags about it, lectures about it, pleads about it, attacks it—in short, when she makes a federal case of it—the behavior only gets worse, often very creatively worse. Mothers finally learn that resistance is not the way to change kids' behavior. But being the least credible people in patriarchy, to ourselves as well as to others, we have a hard time believing that we, in our lowly kitchens, have stumbled upon a principle of human interaction that has cosmic implications.

Talking to my friends that day about disengaging, part of what I knew was that if I were serious about "disappearing" patriarchy, I could never again work to get laws passed in the system. I finally understood that men, who own all laws—since they make, interpret, and enforce them—will never manipulate their legal system in a way that threatens their privilege.

I remembered what happens when women finally *do* persuade men to pass laws for us: how women's hard work in California, for instance, finally produced a no-fault divorce law that, though it quickly proved disastrous for them, they couldn't get rid of because it was so profitable for men; how women in many states, by dint of extraordinary dedication and labor, got child support payment laws passed only to see them succeed primarily for men in extorting child support from *women*; how the same holds true for custody laws—men are using the laws we worked for to take our children away from *us*. Men use the laws we get them to pass as daggers to stab us in the back. How many lessons do we need before we learn the simple facts of gender-based control? I have decided not to be an accomplice in my own oppression any longer, never again to hand men weapons with which to kill me.

Often when I say that laws are not worth warm spit[5] in patriarchy, those women who are frightened by the revolutionary implications of that statement often counter with the argument that *Roe v. Wade* is incontrovertible evidence that women *can* go through men and their system to win freedom. I reply that, unfortunately, *Roe v. Wade* is incontrovertible evidence not of freedom but instead of one of the most blatant co-optations, or re-enslavements, of women by patriarchy in its history. I go on to tell them how I think *Roe v. Wade* saved and continues to serve patriarchy.

I wasn't a feminist at the beginning of the second wave of feminism in this country in the late 60s and early 70s, but I have talked with hundreds of women who were. From them and from the literature written then, I can almost *feel* the incredible excitement of the Movement in those days. Despite, or perhaps partly because of, very legitimate and healthful anger, women were fairly bursting with energy and enthusiasm. Euphoria and elation might best describe the general atmosphere. It was a very heady time. Every woman I have spoken to who was an active feminist then looks back at that time with nostalgia:

---

[5] Suzette Haden Elgin's so-apt phrase in her short story, "Lo, How An Oak Ere Blooming," *Fantasy and Science Fiction*, February 1986, p. 109.

19

those were the halcyon days, the Golden Age.

There were many reasons for that feeling but chief among them, it seems to me, was that liberation seemed not only possible, but imminent. In addition, many feminists had a basic understanding of women's enslavement that has since been lost in a general way: that women are men's colonized lands; that just as the English "colonized"—a racist euphemism for con-quered—Nigeria and India, for instance, men have colonized women. The English declared themselves owners of these countries and their people, made all the laws that governed them, and pocketed the profits themselves. Britannia "ruled" by plundering and raping the colonials and their lands.

The Indians, the Nigerians, the other "colonized" peoples of the world (and colonization takes firmest hold in the feelings and perceptions of a people) tried to make the usurpers' system work for them. They struggled to get laws passed that would give them more leeway, and they managed in some instances to infiltrate low- and even middle-level government echelons and to attain a few managerial and supervisory jobs in the industrial/corporate world. A token handful got into the educational institutions reserved for the masters. Some of them regarded these inroads as progress.

But enough of them eventually realized that it did not matter what else they seemed to achieve, if they did not have home rule, they could never be free. They came to the understanding that freedom was simply not possible for them—ever—in the colonial system. Freedom meant owning themselves, owning their own lands, using their resources for their own enrichment, making their own laws. The revolution began with their feelings and perceptions of themselves as people who not only *should* but *could* govern themselves.

Women were the first owned, the first "ruled" people in every race and class and nation, the first slaves, the first colonized people, the first occupied countries. Many thousands of years ago men took our bodies as their lands as they felt befitted their naturally superior, god-like selves and our lowly, animalistic natures. Since this take-over, they have made all the laws that governed our lands, and have harvested us—our labor, our children, our sexuality, our emotional, spiritual, and cultural richness, our resources of intelligence, passion, devotion—for their own purposes and aggrandizement. These have been men's most profitable cash crops.

Occasionally, some feminist objects to my insistence that men literally own women. I usually discover that as she was growing up her family were Protestants—e.g., Methodist, Presbyterian—or Unitarians, or atheists, or liberals of some stripe, and that therefore as a child and young woman she didn't hear with her actual ears the sort of propaganda those of us reared in Fundamentalist religions heard.

I remember clearly, for instance, visiting girl cousins in another town when I was little and taking a bath with one of them under her mother's supervision. As we were washing, my aunt carefully instructed us not to touch our genitals but instead to spread our legs and with one hand

21

repeatedly splash water upon them. When we asked her why, since that seemed a very ineffective way of getting clean, she answered that we had to save those parts for our husbands, for marriage.

My husband at the time was about five years old and living in Wisconsin. I'm sure he had no interest whatever in the fact that he owned some little girl's reproductive organs in Utah. But I can remember the feeling that experience gave me about my relationship with my body, and I can best describe it as housesitting until the landlord comes home. When one is housesitting someone else's property, one does not rummage through his private things, intimately handle his personal possessions. One behaves circumspectly, carefully, respecting the invisible "no trespassing" signs.

After my speech at the International Women's Book Fair in Montreal in the summer of 1988, Margaret Hecimovich, a young ex-Catholic woman from the midwestern United States, told me that her childhood conditioning had been much fiercer even than mine. When she was a little girl, she was forbidden to *see* herself naked, even in the bathtub. Saving herself for her future lord and master, she washed her body under cover of a long flannel nightgown.

Although most women apparently did not hear the words spoken, every woman born gets the message subliminally, repeatedly and strongly, from her earliest days that she does not belong to herself. And the evidence that we have believed it until now has been our acceptance that men had a right to control our bodies and our lives. Every time we lobbied them for the right to choose whether or not we will have children, we acknowledged that men owned us.

The burgeoning women's health movement of the early 70s was evidence of women's awareness of our physical colonization and of our realization that no matter what else we did, no matter how many laws we got men to pass, no matter how many low-echelon government and corporate positions we won, like the Nigerians and the Indians and all other colonized peoples, unless we had home rule, everything else we did to try to free ourselves was meaningless.

So we were saying "howdy" to our cervixes for the first time in our lives, our own and our friends'. We may have been the 17th person to see them and the first 16 may have been men, but finally we were meeting them face to face. In doing so, we realized that it didn't take a man's eye to see a woman's cervix, it didn't take an American-Medical-Association, male-trained mind to diagnose the health of our reproductive organs or to treat them. We were shocked to remember how "natural" it had seemed to go to male gynecologists, and realized that, in fact, men's being gynecologists was *perverted*, gross, and sick and that our accepting them as experts on our bodies—when they had never had so much as one period in their lives, never experienced one moment of pre-menstrual psychic clarity, never had one birth pain, never suckled one child—was evidence of our ferocious internalized colonization. It began to appear as obscene to us as it truly is.

As obvious as this may seem now, it hadn't *been* obvious for a very long time.

So in learning to examine our own sexual organs, to diagnose and treat our own cervical and vaginal ailments, to do simple abortions, to deliver babies, and in beginning to think seriously about developing our own safe, effective, natural contraceptives and getting the word out, women were moving out of colonization, out of slavery. We were taking back and learning to govern our own countries.

In those days, the movement was called The Women's Liberation Movement, and that, in fact, was what it was. Women were breaking the contract that exists between all oppressed people and their oppressors, in our case our agreement to allow men to own us and to exploit us as their resources. Though we agreed to it under the severest duress imaginable,[6] in order, we thought, to survive, we nevertheless agreed.

Those who do not understand how the thirst for home rule among women at the beginning of the second wave of our Movement in this century rocked the foundations

[6] It is instructive about men that they call the three hundred years in European history during which they massacred nine million women the "Renaissance." The inquisition concluded the process of taming women. Until now we have been good draft horses as Marilyn Fry so brilliantly points out to us in *The Politics of Women's Reality: Essays in Feminist Theory* (The Crossing Press: Trumansburg, NY, 1983, p. 58) and good prostitutes in our marriages, our churches, and our political systems. But now as fear leaves our hearts, the fires of our passion and power have space to blaze unimpeded *inside* us. Our sisters the elements are at last able to befriend and aid us, instead of as in former times made to turn against and destroy us, as all things female and biophilic have been terrorized to turn against and destroy one another.

of patriarchy worldwide simply do not understand the necessity of women's slavery to every level of men's global system. Perhaps even many of the women at that time did not fully understand the revolutionary nature of what they were about. But in establishing a new order in which women owned our own bodies and were not men's property, they were destroying the very foundation of patriarchy. Since any power-over paradigm is totally dependent upon those on the bottom agreeing to stay there, men's world organization was in grave peril. If women would not be slaves, men could not be masters.

The men who control the world are not intelligent, as is evident to even the most casual observer, but they are crafty, particularly about maintaining privilege through control. Over their thousands of years of tyranny, they have acquired a near-perfect understanding of the psychology of the oppressed—if not consciously, then viscerally. They knew precisely what to do when women began refusing to honor the old contract, and I am absolutely convinced that their move was conscious, plotted, and deliberate.

They sent an emissary after the women as they were moving out of the old mind into a free world. Hurrying after us, he shouted, "Hey, girls! Wait up a minute! Listen! You don't need to go to all this trouble. We already know how to do all the things you're having to learn. We know your bodies and what is good for you better than you do. Trying to learn what we already know will take too much of your time and energy away from all your other important '*issues*.'"

25

Then he used men's most successful lie, the hook we had always taken in the past because men are our children and we need to believe they value us, that we can trust them. "You know we love you and want your movement to succeed," he crooned. "So do you know what we're prepared to do for you? If you'll come back, we'll *let* you have legalized abortion!"

How could we refuse such a generous, loving offer? We had listened to men's voices and trusted them for so long—in the face of massive evidence that they had never been trustworthy, had had so little practice in hearing and trusting our own, that we lost our tenuous bearings in the new world and turned around and walked right back into our jail cell. We allowed them to reduce liberation to an "issue." We forgot that anybody that can *let* you, *owns* you.

So the men let us have legalized abortion. Some women protest that women *won* the right to it, forgetting that the legal system is set up to keep patriarchy intact, which means to keep women enslaved, and that men *own* the law. They will never use it to free us. As Audre Lorde states clearly, "The master's tools will never dismantle the master's house."[7]

You know how pityingly we have looked at the benighted woman who says, "I don't need the Women's Movement. My husband *lets* me do anything I want." But our pity has been hypocritical: *Roe v. Wade*, the

---

[7] Audre Lorde, essay by that name in *Sister Outsider*. The Crossing Press: Freedom, CA 1984, p. 110.

"glory" of the movement, is exactly the same sad phenomenon—our husband the state *letting* us, and our feeling grateful for it. But, of course, like a husband the men "let" us not because it is good for us but because it is necessary for them. It keeps us colonized, our bodies state property and our destinies in their hands, and it rivets our attention on them.

So the men let us have legalized abortion, and almost instantly the energy drained from the movement, like air from a punctured balloon. Instead of the Women's Liberation Movement, we became simply the Women's Movement, because liberation is antithetical to letting men, *depending* upon men to, make the laws that govern our lands. For the last 15 years we have been nailed to the system by *Roe v. Wade*, our mighty energy and hope and love channeled into begging men in dozens of state and national bodies not to pare away cent by cent the truly miserable allowance they promised us for abortions for poor women.

If we hadn't trusted them again, if we had kept on going in the direction we were headed, with the same time and money and energy we have since expended on groveling, we could by this time have had a woman on every block in every city and town who is an expert on contraceptives, women's health, birthing, and abortion. We could have educated the women of this country in countless creative ways about their bodies and their right to rule them. We would have learned how to govern ourselves, discovering a whole new way for women—and therefore everyone—to be human.

27

And, significantly, a Bork could have been appointed to every seat of the Supreme Court, men could have been spewing laws aimed at controlling our bodies out of every legal orifice, and all their flailing and sputtering would simply be irrelevant. Having removed ourselves from their jurisdiction, we would have settled the question of abortion and birth control, of women's individual freedom, blessedly and for ages to come. When the Nigerians and Indians got ready to rule themselves, the English had no choice but to go home. Tyranny is a contract. Both parties have to stick to it.

But in the early 70s women hadn't had time to complete the necessary internal revolution in how we thought and felt about ourselves that was necessary for us to be free. Evidence of this is that we took as models for our movement the movements that had preceded ours, all of which were reformist because they involved men. Since our own internal, authentic women's voices were still very weak and difficult to hear and when heard still without sufficient authority, we didn't take seriously enough the fact that women and men are in wildly different relationships to the system. We didn't realize that since the entire global system of laws and governments is set up with the primary purpose of keeping women of every color and class enslaved by men of their own color and class, and often by other men as well, talking about civil rights for women was oxymoronic. We had still to learn how colossally brainwashed we are by patriarchy to do in the name of freedom precisely those things that will further enslave us.

Roe v. Wade was very smart politics for the men; now, regardless of what party is in power or who is on the Supreme Court, the groundwork has been laid. The hopes of thousands of dedicated feminists are bound firmly once more to the husband-state. And we are all a dozen years further away from trusting women and finding a lasting non-male-approval-based solution to the problem of our physical and emotional colonization.

It is time for us to remember that no one can free us but ourselves. Time not to try to get the men to do it for us—which reinforces their illusion of godhood and ours of wormhood and perpetuates the deadly power-over model of reality—but to do it ourselves. Time for thousands of us to learn to perform abortions and to do all that needs to be done for one another in so many neighborhoods throughout the country that our liberation cannot be stopped. Time to manage our own bodies, heal our own bodies, own our own bodies. It is time for home rule.

This is how I want women to spend our prodigious intelligence and energy.

Obviously, *Roe v. Wade* doesn't stand alone; it simply models patriarchy's subversive tactics most clearly.[8] Almost all segments of our Movement have suffered such co-optation. Many women who have been active in the shelter movement for years, for instance, have pointed out to me the similarities in strategy and effect between *Roe*

---

[8] I use war terms such as "strategy" and "tactic" only when talking about actual war, as I am here in addressing men's war against women.

v. Wade and government funding for shelters.

To obtain funding for shelters in the first place, women must tone down their feminism and conform to male officials' standards and expectations. To keep the money, the women who work in the shelters as well as those who come there for help are required to do masses of paper work, the purpose of which seems to be to keep women from helping and receiving help. In some areas, when women are in crisis and call a shelter, before their feelings and needs can even be addressed they must be asked a dozen questions and informed at length about the conditions under which the shelter will accept them (they can have no weapons, for instance).[9] Many women simply hang up in total frustration and anger. In other instances, funders won't allow discussions of racism or homophobia or of battering among Lesbians. They also often control who is hired. Funders regularly split women's organizations apart by clouding the issues of who is going to define the group, what their work is, what their analysis is, and even what the issue is.[10]

In addition, nearly every funder's prerequisites are designed to keep women powerless, thinking and behaving as victims. One state, for example, requires

[9] I learned much about this situation in a meeting with women law students in Madison, Wisconsin, April, 1988.

[10] Suzanne Pharr, director of the Women's Project in Little Rock, Arkansas, "Do we want to play faust with the government? Or, how do we get our social change work funded and not sell our souls?" speech at the March 1987 National Lesbian and Gay Health Conference in Los Angeles.

shelters to use only professional counselors, specifically prohibiting peer counseling. Peer counseling, I am told by women with much experience, is the only counseling that has yet been seen to have any significant effect upon battered women.

Because of the scope and depth of the subversion of our purposes by funders, local and national, many shelter workers agree with Suzanne Pharr who concluded her brave speech at the 1987 National Lesbian and Gay Health Conference in Los Angeles with these words: "From my experience, my strongest urge is to say, DO ANYTHING—BEG, BORROW, STEAL—BUT DON'T TAKE GOVERNMENT FUNDING!"[11]

Trapped in the victim/rescuer/persecutor loop,[12] we continue to believe that men will rescue us—even knowing that among the men who grant funds for shelters and rape crisis lines are many who rape and brutalize their wives, daughters, and other women. "But that's just the point," some women expostulate. "Those are precisely the ones who *should* be paying for shelters!" But we can never forget for a moment that such men will only pay guilt money in a way that ensures their violent access to women. I think we have to be constantly aware that, like other colonized people, we cannot get free, we cannot change our oppressed reality, through the colonists'

[11] Suzanne Pharr, speech at the March 1987 National Lesbian and Gay Health Conference.

[12] Diana Rabenold, *Love, Politics, and "Rescue" in Lesbian Relationships,* Lesbian-Feminist Essay Series, No. 2, HerBooks: Santa Cruz, CA.

system.

"Well, then, Sonia," women say to me at this point, "if trying to change laws, or to amend the Constitution [the greatest document for freedom *for men* in the history of the world], and if civil disobedience and protests and lobbying and campaigns and voting[13] aren't the ways to change reality, then what *is*? What *shall* we do?"

[13] Women didn't even *get* the vote until it no longer mattered. One of the major characteristics of a hierarchy is that it goes pyramidally up and up until there are only a few at the top. A handful of men—totally behind the scenes—already owned the world by 1920 and no matter who anyone voted for after that, those few men won. As the bumper sticker sums it up, "If voting could change things, it would be illegal."

CHAPTER 2

A Better *Today*

After the demise of the ERA in June 1982, everywhere I went in this country women were asking desperately, "What shall we do *now*? What shall we *do*?" a relentless refrain that over the next few years took on a peculiarly nightmarish quality for me; I heard it in my dreams, echoing off the walls and along the corridors of my mind. If I had believed in myself and other women seriously enough then, it would have taken me only a short time to figure out that it was the wrong question, and why. The clue was that *we couldn't answer it.* Women are brilliant, individually and together. If we couldn't answer it, it had to be because it was not answerable; it had to be that it was the wrong question.

As I thought about that, I began to understand that it was an unanswerable question because we can't postulate a new paradigm standing in and saturated by the old one.

How, for instance, can we devise plans, how can we even *imagine* what women would do if we were free of patriarchy—free in the cells of our bodies, our genes and chromosomes, every atom of our brains? We haven't seen women feel and act free for over 5,000 years. Even if we could remember back before patriarchy, there has never been a time on this planet when women have been in the situation we are now in, so even our species' memory contains no model. The only way we are going to know how free women behave is to become free ourselves and watch our own behavior. Only then can we say with authority, "*This* is what free women do!"

But in the meantime, we can't think from bondage into freedom, we can't ask, "What should we *do*?" because if we do, we have none but the old conditioned answers; the horizons of our imaginations are limited by our old blinders.

We *can* think, however, "How do I want to feel, how do I want to *be* in the new world?" It took me four years of thinking about it almost continually to reach the conclusion that those were the relevant questions, the questions answerable in non-collaborative, change-effect-ing terms: "how shall we *be*? How shall we feel about ourselves? What kind of a world do we want for ourselves *right now*?" It took me another year to understand *why* those are the relevant questions and why resistance is profoundest collaboration. It took women's insistence that I explain myself more fully, that I offer more satisfactory reasoning for the conclusions I had reached with intuitive leaps. Through the whole process, I learned that if I could ask the right question, the answer followed almost at once.

Working to clarify my theory, I remembered that shortly after I became a feminist in 1977, I attended a feminist event where I heard an idea that made tears of relief pour down my cheeks and that now seems to me basic to any discussion of how to make the new world we long for. The woman speaking said, "A fundamental feminist principle is that the means are the ends; that *how* we do something is *what* we get."

The tears of relief were from realizing that I wasn't stupid after all and I have since figured out why I had always thought I was, how much of my life-long feeling of alienation that principle explains.

I went through the entire male educational system feeling intellectually inferior to men, as if a part of my brain weren't functioning. I endured countless agonizing moments of being terrified that others would see through my disguise of intelligence to my true witlessness.

I remember sitting in one graduate seminar after another, the men in their tweed jackets with leather elbows, pulling on their pipes—English departments are incredibly stuffy—talking, as I trusted then, eruditely about their ideas, taking themselves very seriously. I felt humble and wormlike in their presence, full of gratitude to be allowed to sit at their feet. But there was often a place in their discussion where reason seemed to skip a beat. At first I would interrupt and say something like, "Uh, Arnold . . . I didn't follow that. Would you please, uh, *recapitulate* a little?"

Every face in the room—and in those days most of the faces were male—would turn slowly toward me. With pained looks everyone would sigh as if to say, "Why did we even allow them to learn to *read*?" A couple of such humiliating scenes was all it took to silence me. After that, when they came to the places in their discourse that I couldn't follow, I simply faked it. Like everyone else in the room, I looked wise and nodded my head and murmured, "Um hum, um hum." Over the years I got so good at faking it that sometimes I'd even nudge the fellow next to me with my elbow and murmur, "Interesting, hmm?"

So I faked my way through a master's program and bluffed my way through a doctorate, thinking the while that everyone else must be very smart to be getting the connection I always seemed to be missing. I got so good at faking it, in fact, that I forgot I *was* faking it. But on some level, I knew I didn't get it at all.[1]

But recently I have come to understand much more fully the implications of what I learned in that feminist gathering that night. Not just that I was right all along, that reason *had* skipped beats, my colleagues *had* missed connections. But more significantly, the reason I hadn't got the point of their arguments was that they *weren't gettable*. The very structure of male thought is faulty.

Now that I have become aware of it, I hear men's

---

[1] Did *you* get why men adore *Moby Dick? M. Dick* is the most boring and pointless book I ever forced myself to read in my life, and that's saying a great deal since I forced myself through tons of their grim "great" books

36

spurious cause-and-effect, goal-oriented, five-year-plan, means-to-ends "reasoning" a dozen times a day. But of the multifarious examples of it, the one that illustrates most clearly how it skews and distorts reality is this:

Men say that, their goal being peace, naturally they are going to have to bomb and bomb and massacre and rape and pillage and torture and lay waste and then—this is the place at which I used to feel as if I were the only person on earth who hadn't caught on—suddenly, miraculously, there will come a magical moment, a moment when some sort of alchemy takes place, and—*voila!*—peace!

Hey guys, run that by me again, will ya?

Women have always known on some level that there is only one way to have peace and that is to be peaceful right now. We have understood that, because the means are the ends, *how* we behave is *what* we get.

But as I thought this idea through time and time again during the last couple of years, I found that it wasn't enough for me that some feminist had once asserted that it was true, or that my intuition—that I call "my wise woman inside"—had shouted, "Yes!" when I'd heard it, or that it explained so much that had been inexplicable. I wanted the theory, the how and the why of it. I wanted to get it with all my faculties, feel more intellectually satisfied with it. I needed to think it through for myself.

I found that the key to understanding it more satisfactorily came from atomic physics, the idea that in our atomic universe there is no such thing as linear time.[2] Atomic science tells us that, contrary to how we have been conditioned to perceive it, time does not move from here to there, it is *not* like a river, it is not "passing," not going anywhere. Instead, it simply *is*, like the ocean, and we are in it as fish are in the sea. Time is our medium. We are at any moment in all the time there ever was or ever will be, surrounded by time in the form, paradoxically, of, at once, only an instant and also eternity.

Because there is no past or future separate from the present (since all time is together here right now), the past and the future exist only in the present. There is not a detached blob of time somewhere out in the ocean called "future ocean," or a partial blip of ocean left behind called "past ocean." Like the ocean, all time is together and now.

This is immensely important for several reasons. For one thing, it means that since this moment is the only time we have, the only time we have the power to change or create anything is right this moment. One of the cruelest crimes of patriarchy has been to teach us to project our thoughts into a future that will never come (getting together our vitae and our five-year-plans) or

---

[2] Like many other women, I am hearing the concepts from atomic physics not as if I am learning them for the first time, but like echoes, like memories—like not-quite-accurate memories. I'm pretty certain from my own experience that during archaic women's times all of us understood and felt time and space and our place in the universe in a completely different way, that men are only now beginning to suspect the existence of that mode of consciousness, that they have so far to go and so much to revise that women must leave them to it and rush on ahead *experiencing* it.

focusing us back into a past that is only memories of a present, keeping us unaware of the locus of our power in the present moment and effectively imprisoning us in time.

But an even more crucial reason for understanding time as an ocean rather than as a river is that if all time is together in this moment, the present and the future are not separate. More than this, since the future is in the birth canal of the present, we can predict the future by what we are doing in the present. What we are doing in the present is *creating* the future, *is* the future.

For me the implications of this are stunning. It answers the question of how we go about making a new world right here in the putrid debris of senile patriarchy: we *do now* what we want to be doing in the future, we *be now*, *feel now* how we thought we could be and feel only in some future time.

This means that if we want a future world in which women are not afraid—of rape and poverty and humiliation and other male violence—there is only one way to create it and that is by being unafraid now. We can't first try to change the men so women don't have to be afraid of them. If we do this now, we make the future one in which women, in fear, continue to try to change men. We can't get to fearlessness from being afraid; a magical moment of alchemy when fearlessness appears is as impossible as peace appearing out of rape and pillage. We make a fear-free world by being unafraid in this moment, the only moment we live.

Because what we are doing and feeling now

determines the future, we can make a world in which women are not sacrificing our time and energy, our needs and desires, for someone else's better world down the line somewhere, by not sacrificing now or ever again.

The wise old woman who lives inside me told me this emphatically in my early days as a feminist, but I didn't take her seriously then. When I first came into the Women's Movement over a decade ago during the ERA campaign, I attended meeting after meeting in which speakers, trying to pump up flagging enthusiasm, said something like, "I know you're exhausted; so am I. We've all been working so diligently and bravely, nearly burning ourselves out. And even though we know we probably won't see the results of our labors in our lifetimes, I for one say it's been worth it. It's been worth it to make sure our children have a better world than we had. So I'm not going to give up, and I know you're not going to either. Right?" And the audience would fairly scream as one, "Right! We'll never give up!"

Though my innards were complaining, "Yuk! I don't want a better tomorrow; I want a better *today*!" I would squish this renegade feeling and shout, "I'll never give up!" right along with everybody else, knowing, none better, that how long you could put off present for greater future gratification was one of patriarchy's prime criteria for true adulthood. I don't believe that any more, of course. Cause and effect, as men have perceived and taught it, simply does not explain my reality and never has. Neither does their hatred and fear of pleasure.

I have also stopped believing the lie that the change

we want takes a very long time and will happen sometime, somewhere out there in the future. I am certain that the future is now, that what men erroneously call "the future" does not exist. Because it does not exist, there can be no cause and effect, no getting there from here. There is simply being there, being now the way we want to be and the way we want women to be in a new world, not doing other "interim" things in some futile effort to *get* there. Doing "interim" things makes a future in which women in vain continue to do "interim" things.

This means that if we want a future world in which women are not on our knees pleading with men to be a little kinder—economically, politically, legally, religiously, personally—we must get up off our knees right now. There is no magic moment when groveling suddenly becomes self-respect and independence of spirit.

Neither is there any moment of alchemy when getting women into office will change the system, because what women have to do today to get into office *determines* what they will be doing in the future. There is simply no getting to a feminist value system by acting out of the old patriarchal values of competition, expediency, hierarchy. Another way of saying that the means are the ends is to point out that we can't touch filth, even while trying to clean it up, without getting it on our hands.

Women say, "But if I can get in there, I can subvert their system for women's ends." But since the only genuinely subversive act for prisoners of war is to get *out*, the very fact of staying *in* prevents a woman from being subversive. Thinking of the women who got "in," I consider that I haven't seen one instance of their subverting the system. Any liberal man could have done as well or better for women since he wouldn't have been seen as not being objective, as favoring his own group. I wonder, when I hear a woman say that *she* will succeed in subversion where others have failed, what makes her think she is the exceptional one? I wonder why we can't honor other women's experience, learn from it, and say, "If they didn't change the system, it's because they couldn't. If being as they are—strong, smart, courageous women—they couldn't do it, it's because it can't be done." Thousands have tried and failed. I suggest we thank them for making clear its futility and move on.

There is no getting to integrity from not having any now, from voting for the least offensive candidates, for instance, knowing that at best their vision is reformist and that reform is collusion. Voting for either men or women in this system is voting *for* the system, for patriarchy, which is based on the hatred of women. So there is no way on earth for self-loving women to vote without compromising our integrity. We are living in the future this moment, creating it breath by breath. What we do and how we do it right now is the world of the future.

Some people were shocked that I didn't vote in the 1988 election. I was shocked that they *did*. The day after, I overheard a conversation on a plane in which one man was lamenting to another: "It seems to me that we never have a decent candidate any more, that we have to vote for the lesser of two evils every time. I can't understand it." If he had realized that by voting for the lesser of two evils, he helped create a world in which he would always have to vote for the lesser of two evils; if he had understood that by voting for evil *at all*, even if for a *lesser* evil, he was still voting for evil, and that since everyone who voted, voted for evil—either a lesser or greater one—surely there was no possible way to get anything *but* evil; if he had understood that what he was doing every moment of his life was determining future moments, he would have been shocked to see his collusion in the deteriorating political situation that he deplored. We cannot compromise our integrity and have a reality with integrity anymore than we can have peace by waging war.

It seems to me, therefore, that if we want a world in which women have integrity and are independent, self-governing, and untamed—and patriarchy cannot survive women's being any of these—we have to have integrity, be independent, self-governing, and wild *right now*. The new world, the feminist world, is not somewhere off in a nonexistent future. That world is either right now or it is never. To the degree that this moment we feel independent of men and their system and do not participate in it, we live in a world where patriarchy cannot exist. Men cannot do patriarchy without our fear and dependence.

I want the new world to be a place in which everyone is guided by the integrity of their own self-loving inner voice all the time. So when the woman under the tree in Michigan asked me if I thought she was being irresponsible, I told her, "You don't have to believe a word *I* say. I could be on the wrong track altogether. You don't need to listen to or believe anyone else on earth. But it seems to me that to have integrity you *must* believe your own voice, the voice that just spoke to you through your body."

Because our bodies cannot be either in the past or in the future as our brains can, but are anchored firmly in the present—the only time we are alive and therefore the only time we have power—they are absolutely trustworthy messengers. Men have tried manfully to disconnect spirit and mind and body to prevent our having integrity, to keep us from piecing together our shattered voice. But the truth is that we are whole—spirit and mind and body intimately interwoven with one another, each existing in and informing the others. When our bodies speak, they make us privy to the intentions of our spirits and deep minds.

Our bodies are easy to understand if we will listen to them and take them seriously. What does that really mean? Many women feel the rightness of what they are thinking and doing affirmed somewhere in their bodies, in the pits of their stomachs, for instance, or in their chests. I experience the "right" or "go" signal very strongly in the high center of my torso, between my abdomen and back ribs, and often simultaneously all over and throughout my body. Sometimes my skin prickles.

I explained further to the woman in Michigan my belief that when we are doing or thinking things that are truly freeing, or when we are being free in some way, we feel free right that moment—light, buoyant, full of hope and energy and love—that's how we know we're on the right track. "When did you expect to feel liberated, and what did you think it was going to feel like?" I demanded of her. "Whatever and whenever, the feeling you just described to me—*this* is *it*, the time and feeling you've been longing and working so hard for and thought was far off in a mythical future somewhere."

When I have this feeling, I hold on to it as long as I can. Its very gloriousness has much to teach me about reality. Anytime I want it back, I remember how I got to it in the first place. I "am" in the present the way I hoped to be sometime in the new feminist world. I practice seeing and feeling the vibrant colors around me, feel the breeze on my skin, breathe deeply and often, touch everything, wake up, come alive, be unafraid, forgive myself, love myself madly, be joyful. Patriarchy cannot exist in the presence of life and joy and fearlessness and love of self, so all the while any of us are experiencing these feelings, we make and hold a space in the cosmos where there is no oppression of women. When enough of us create such a space inside and around ourselves, when enough of us feel free of the imperatives of this system, moment by moment, freedom will become reality for all women in the world.

The principle that the means are the ends provides more—and more conclusive—evidence that resistance is not only futile, but that it literally and actively strengthens the things resisted. Our failure to understand this principle earlier explains to me why the Women's Movement has not yet created a new world, let alone transformed the old one. I understand now why women's resistance—our protesting, demonstrating, lobbying, demanding—did not and cannot change patriarchy.

Resistance is the other, essential half of the war model: attack/resist; it takes both attack and resistance together to make war. Resistance, therefore, *is* war, and since the means are the ends, war can only produce more war, never peace.

The bumper sticker says it all: "What if they threw a war and nobody came?" The men are still throwing the age-old, all-out, global, gynecidal war against women, but I'm not going, and if I don't go, they can't use my resistance to keep the war going. If enough of us don't go, they can't throw the war at all. I want women everywhere not to go to the war anymore. I want us not to turn up on the battlefield thinking we can win when we can only be slaughtered.

For this reason, I no longer think of myself as a "woman warrior" as I once did. I am not fighting anything or anyone anymore, not mimicking men's old deadly pattern. I think of myself and other like-minded women now as the goddess,[3] creating a new pattern, creating the world afresh.

As soon as enough of us—and it doesn't need the majority, just the critical mass of us—feel right now how we thought we were going to feel down the road sometime when the men had changed and when bit by bit

---

[3] I explain what I mean by this in my book, *Going Out of Our Minds: The Metaphysics of Liberation,* The Crossing Press: Freedom, CA, 1987, Chapter 1.

we had knocked down the patriarchal fortress, the moment the small number that is the critical mass of us is able to live moment by moment in the new mind, that is the moment when that mind will become the general mind of the planet. Living in that world is the way it can become reality, in the same way that living in the patriarchal mind moment by moment has been keeping patriarchy real. Just as there is no way to have peace but to be peaceful right now, there is no way to have joy, fearlessness, and freedom except to feel them right now.

From these feelings will come behavior that will move us into a reality organic to those feelings, consonant with them. Acting out of feelings of self-worth, for instance, we immediately create a world in which we are worthy. We can tell when we truly love and respect and honor ourselves because we are no longer able to behave like slaves. We do not have to plan how not to; we simply find that when we respect ourselves we cannot, for instance, beg men, cannot lobby them. Appropriate new behavior comes out of appropriate new feelings.

Acting out of fearlessness, we create a world in which we do not need to be afraid. As Elsa Gidlow says, "My observation is that the Lesbians who suffer are the ones unsure within themselves, always fearing they will be condemned. *They thus attract what they dread* [italics added], as weakness cruelly invites and encourages the bully." [4]

---

[4] Elsa Gidlow, *Elsa: I Come With My Songs*. Booklegger Press: San Francisco, 1986, p. 252.

Acting with integrity, we create a world in which we can be whole. We know when we have integrity because we are unable to compromise ourselves, and we can monitor our internal revolution by how much we are able to participate in the present woman-hating system. Future reality is transformed when we change our feelings about ourselves—and hence our behavior—in the present.

So if we want a world in which women love and trust ourselves and one another, *right now* we must feel that love and trust. Women's learning to respect and honor women is the basis of a spiritual revolution that is changing what it means to live as human beings on Earth.

The old saying that tomorrow never comes is literally and absolutely true. If we want a feminist world, there is only this moment to have it in.

A couple of deeply entrenched bits of conditioning make my practicing this theory, my living in this new place moment by moment, very difficult. Generalizing as usual from a sample of one, I assume that if these are troublesome for me, they are troublesome for many other women.

One of these pervasive messages is that change can only come about through struggle, that we aren't making any difference unless we're batting our heads against concrete walls, unless it's all very difficult and we are miserable. We've been taught, in fact, that we can gauge how much change we're making by how much we're suffering.

I can't think of a better example of patriarchal reversal because the truth is exactly the opposite: all we can get by struggle, by pain and misery, is more struggle, more pain, and more misery. But because of our socialization, we have a hard time *feeling*—though we may believe it—that anything as wonderful as feeling wonderful can possibly bring a new reality into being. That out of feeling wonderful will emerge *action* of such transcendent difference, brilliance, and power that we cannot begin to imagine it.

Our inability to accept this is largely a matter of guilt—feeling guilty for not suffering when others *are*. This is the other recalcitrant chunk of conditioning. Surely if we feel joyous and free while all over the world so many of our sisters are wretched, we must be racist and classist and ageist and able-bodiest—we must not care about anybody but ourselves.

Diana Rabenold addresses this when she writes:

> The *fact* of women's subordination as a group becomes internalized in individual women as a belief that their personal needs are not important: that to ask for what they want or to get their needs met is selfish, that they are only good and OK if they always put the needs of others first. Indeed, the accusation of "selfishness"—however subtly communicated—has ironically been perhaps the greatest barrier to women's development of a strong sense of Self with which to *be* "Self-ish!" [5]

Elsa Gidlow, working-class woman, life-long Lesbian,

---

[5] Diana Rabenold, *Love, Politics, and "Rescue" in Lesbian Relationships*, p. 5.

puts it this way:

> Have you ever wakened to the realization that you were happy? It's hard to put into words where it comes from, the sudden awareness that the day is somehow transformed by radiance. Like this morning. . . . why am I visited by this sense of all being well? All is not well, as every newscaster will tell us. Should I listen? Or shall I allow the uninvited happiness to illumine the day while outdoors the rain incontinently pours down and everywhere people suffer? Do I have a right to it? . . . Must we *deserve* a rainbow? [6]

The answer is yes, that's what we've been taught, that we must "deserve" a rainbow, that we get the rainbow only if we work for it, struggle for it, suffer for it, sacrifice enough for others. But the truth is that our simply being alive, simply being *us* gives us a right to rainbows, and it is neither necessary nor useful to continue to try to *earn* happiness by rescuing first everyone else who is suffering.

Women have asked me if I mean that if we all just go sit in our hot tubs and think about our careers and be contented, everything will come right with the world. I was on a NOW panel with a friend who couldn't resist a little jab at "those who believe we should just contemplate our navels."

I'm always surprised by such misunderstanding, perhaps since I know that all my thought and behavior is

[6] Elsa Gidlow, *Elsa: I Come With My Songs,* p. 306.

focused upon bringing into existence an actual new global society, that this is what I believe women are here to do, the reason we were born, and that this is anything *but* passive. In fact, I'm hard pressed to think of more radical action than this.

Perhaps one of the reasons for the misunderstanding is that what I am saying seems to echo the political contextlessness and passivity of the New Age Movement, a movement that daily subverts the Women's Movement and steals adherents from it by mimicking women's culture, by glossing the surface with woman-like rhetoric while seething underneath with the same old misogyny. The fact and history of male domination of women and of *any* oppression and suffering is denied and erased under the headings of "Be Here Now!" and "Whatever is, is right!"

My daughter, Kari, tells me on the telephone that a great deadness has fallen upon the town where she lives since so many people are living lives with no politics, no context, no history—New Age lives. One day as she and an acquaintance were talking on the street, a man walked by, eyed Kari up and down and said suggestively, "Hey, Chick!" Bored, not even turning to look at him, she told him to "fuck off." Her friend was shocked. "If you were living in the present," she said, "you could see that that guy, deep down, is really a fine person. Why can't you take it that way?" The idea that living in the moment means that whatever is, is right, that there is no history, no context for behavior, is wrong-headed and dangerous hocus-pocus.

The New Age concept of "being here now" seems to me grossly reductionist, reducing the moment to its smallest, most drastically exclusive denominator, as if it is all there is of history, of truth, even of sensory possibility. In this process, everything—all acts, thoughts, and perceptions—becomes totally relative and of equal importance, equal good, and judgment becomes an undesirable, even antisocial, act.

When I speak of living in this moment, I am not talking about living any old way and saying that any way is as good as any other way. I am not speaking of ignoring or denying political reality, oppression and pain. I am saying that we must live *as if* we were free, *as if* we were in every way the women we have dreamed of becoming, *as if* the world were as we wish it to be, and in saying that, I preserve history, provide context, expand the moment to its largest inclusiveness, I make judgment a moral necessity, I imply transcendence.

The suffering of the women of the world, past and present, has haunted my waking hours and my dreams since the night I woke to it in a Mormon church meeting, the night a dozen years ago that I became a feminist. I have not forgotten their suffering for a single second since. But I have had to face the difficult truth that all the things women have done to try to make the system work for them only made matters worse: every statistic describing violence against women has soared in the last 20 years; the government itself tells us that by the year 2,000 the entire poverty population of the United States of America will be women and our children.

I for one am no longer willing to keep on doing harmful things for selfish reasons—to keep my conscience comfortably salved or to prove to others that I really care about women. Regardless of any risk to either my conscience or to my reputation, I am determined to make a world and live in it right now in which violence against women is unthinkable, in which poverty for women and children is unthinkable. I understand now why we can't stop these in the ways we've tried up to now, and I can't bear to keep on making them worse.

The best I know to do is to invite all women of every race and class, every age, every sexual proclivity, every physical endowment, who are looking for another way, all women who can't stand the ugly vicious system one moment longer to join me and thousands of other women in this country in making a new world. And I mean this literally: *to make a new world—physically, economically, socially, in every way.* I am determined above all else to try to live feminism, as I understand it better daily, and to live *in* feminism every moment precisely because I *do* care, precisely because I *do* love women. I know I can't free anyone but myself, but my inner voice tells me that in freeing myself, I make freedom more accessible to all other women.

The assumption that we show true concern, real love, by trying to rescue others is a particularly perverse patriarchal tenet—another reversal. "Rescue" is the other side of "victim," essential to it, a component part. There must be rescuers for there to be victims, and visa versa. Some say white women are racist if we do not continue to try to rescue the women of color in the ghettos of our cities and of the world. But the Lady Bountiful attitude of white women in believing that women of color need us to rescue them, that they can't do what they need to do for themselves—*that* kind of condescension and need to control others is what seems to me to be racist.[7]

What I hear women of color saying to me is that what I can do for them—and for myself—is to wrest racism out of my soul. To make the space inside and around me nonracist space, adding this space to the other nonracist spaces on the planet until ultimately that is the space that prevails.

I don't hear them asking me to take care of them; as far as I can see, they neither need nor want me to. Women of color the world over are freeing themselves in most amazing ways, and their rising is the very foundation of the global Women's Movement, the single most significant and transformative event of this age. I can be grateful to them, I can listen to them, and I can support them in every way open to me, I can care and love and applaud, and when I can, give of my resources.

---

[7] I am not suggesting that all "helping" activities are "rescue": useless and/or collaborative. Teaching women in Nicaragua, for instance, how to build their own houses, or set up clinics, helps all women involved to discover their power. I *am* suggesting, though, that unless we are fully conscious as we participate in them that we cannot rescue anyone, that unless each Nicaraguan women does her own internal revolution, these activities will not only *not* change the world but will ultimately aid the patriarchs of Nicaragua, who still own the women and all they produce. We need also to remember that if we do not attend to our own personal internal revolutions at the same time that we are helping others, we are not really helping anyone, either ourselves, the women of Nicaragua, or any other of the women of the world.

But I can't make the system work for them. It's just not going to work for women of *any* color or class.

I have given up rescuing so that I do not help create victims. I am not even trying to save the world any more, not even focused on trying to save myself. I am simply determined to find freedom, right now, by changing myself. As my friend A. E. Dropper puts it:

> It means that the world as one knows it falls apart completely when you change yourself. For a radical feminist, patriarchy falls apart. And a few years down the road you might try to get patriarchy back for the sake of making conversation with a radical feminist in your kitchen, and damned if you can't get it back. But you can't. It's a little dizzying, but you can't forget that you haven't suffered for awhile, and that all your days and nights are filled with meaning. (Correspondence, December 11, 1987.)

What I am doing now is walking by the side of any woman who is traveling in my direction, listening to her ideas about how we can practice being free, sharing with her the fullness of my heart at having her company in this greatest of all human journeys, the journey to transcendence that never ends, widening and clearing the path as we walk, clearing resting places.

Sometimes women quote the well-known "When they came for the Jews" passage[8] as evidence that we must

---

[8] Attributed to Martin Niemoeller, the entire quote is: In Germany they came first for the communists and I didn't speak up because I wasn't a communist. Then they came for the Jews and I didn't speak up because I wasn't a Jew. Then they came for the trade unionists and I didn't speak up

rescue others in danger or else when our turn comes no one will come to our aid. They give the necessity to stop the Hitlers of the world as one reason why we must fight wars. To these women I reply:

Every day patriarchy comes for *you* again, to get your mind and heart again, to destroy you, body and soul. If you cannot extricate yourself from its grasp, if you are imprisoned, how can you expect to free anyone else? The first step is to get free ourselves in all the ways we know are necessary. And as we break free, we make a hole in the paradigm that others can escape through with us. Somehow, in ways we're just beginning to glimpse, we help make liberation possible for everyone when we liberate ourselves.

When we free ourselves, we destroy patriarchy at the root. Trying to clip off its buds has not been successful. In stopping Hitler, we did not in any way impede the propensity for patriarchy to produce Hitlers; there is now a potential Hitler on every street corner. In fact, in fighting against Hitler, others became like him. Though Hitler is responsible for millions of hideous deaths, every country that fought him also killed millions of innocent people in terrible ways. In trying to stop a tyrant, they had to become tyrants. We become what we resist.

None of this means that we should stand by while others are hurt and not do what we can, but if resistance

---

because I wasn't a trade unionist. Then they came for the Catholics and I didn't speak up because I was a Protestant. They came for me and by that time no one was left to speak up.

is the most powerful collaboration, the question is, how can we truly help and not hinder?

Denmark approached this problem with exquisite creativity. Not to hide the Jews—because in hiding them they would have made a world where Jews must be hidden in order to be safe—but to make Jewishness extra visible: every Dane to wear a yellow Star of David, every Dane to be a Jew. If enough countries had done this, there would have come into being a world in which being visible as a Jew would be the greatest safety.

This was not civil disobedience, it was not resistance; it was living in the kind of world right then that they wanted to have in the future.

It is women's destiny to create a world in which Hitler is unthinkable and therefore impossible. Another world, right now, right here, a safe, joyous, healthful, loving place, *home* for our species and all other living things. This is what I think we are about, those of us women fortunate enough to live at this time. Often during my speeches I ask the women in the room who feel as if they were born to do an immense work of great consequence to raise their hands. More than half always do and I suspect that the ones who don't very likely would if I were to ask them again in a few years.

I take women seriously. If we feel that we came specifically at this time to work wonders, I trust that that *is* why we came. And I trust that one of those wonders will be our leaving the patriarchal state in smoking ruins behind us, reduced to ashes by our passion for freedom.

CHAPTER 3

The Great Divorce

A s I have talked to slightly bewildered audiences across the country about women's relationship with the patriarchal state, trying to make clear what I thought we ought to do about it and why, a way of understanding and expressing it more clearly has come to me. Earlier, I had recognized that the system behaved—in the case of *Roe v. Wade*, for example—in the same manner toward women generally as one husband behaves specifically toward one wife. My seeing this brought women's situation in patriarchy into much sharper focus.

All women are battered women in patriarchy. Every woman born is in an abusive relationship with men as a class and with their system since the raison d'etre of all men's institutions—political, legal, educational, religious, economic, and social—is to achieve and perpetuate the slavery of women and the dominion of men. Therefore, if we can understand why one woman stays in an abusive relationship with one man[1]—and the Women's Movement has taught us much about this—we can understand why women as a caste stay in our abusive relationship with the state. It follows that if we can understand what it takes for one woman to extricate herself permanently from a battering situation, we can understand what it will take for *all* women to extricate ourselves permanently from patriarchy—our brutal relationship with men as a class. Finally, if we can understand what happens to a marriage when a woman finally and unequivocally leaves it, we can predict what will happen when women finally and unequivocally leave our marriage with our husband the state.

Many of us grew up watching our fathers abuse our mothers—physically or emotionally or both—and were filled with confusion and rage. We couldn't understand why they took it, why they didn't just *leave*. Standing outside our mothers' situations, we could see that they had options, reasonable options, and we assumed that they could see them too.

What we have learned since, however, from our own sad experience or from listening to other women's stories, is that in the midst of cruelty, many women really cannot see any way out; as far as they are aware, they have no choices. They are trapped in the invisible reality of their feelings and perceptions and beliefs.

---

[1] Although some women are in abusive relationships with other women, the model is the male/female relationship.

How does a woman lose her consciousness of alternatives? What are the mechanisms that have to come into play not only to make her believe that she is choice-less but also to weld her so tightly to her aggressor that leaving him seems life threatening?

On the most overt level is what I call SHATTER— Self-Hatred and Terror—the continuing education program her husband or husband-surrogate subjects her to in his capacity as agent-in-place for the male hegemony. His job is to reinforce and intensify the conditioning of her other intensive trainers—the media, her parents, ministers, teachers, society in general. In this guerrilla warfare against her, he has global male culture as his model, his authority, his back-up, and his resource.

Though not every abusive husband employs all the following indoctrination and intimidation tactics, most must use many of them to achieve the desired effect. A man intent on dehumanizing a woman, for instance, often tries to isolate her, to control what she does, who she sees and talks to, and where she goes. He may harass her economically by trying to prevent her from getting or keeping a job, making her ask for money, giving her an allowance, or taking any money she makes. He is likely to force her into sexual acts against her will, attacking the sexual parts of her body, raping her, and generally treating her as a sex object. And, of course, physical abuse is standard: he beats her, throws her down, twists her arms, trips, bites, pushes, shoves, slaps, chokes, pulls her hair, punches, kicks, grabs, and/or uses a weapon against her.[2]

He is busy at the same time with verbal strategies, humiliating, scapegoating, and threatening her. He tells her that she is stupid and disgusting, barely fit to be his servant; that she's lucky she's got him because no one else would have her, he's better than she deserves, any other man would treat her worse; that she needs him to make the rules and important decisions because she is incompetent and would botch everything; that she's responsible for his bad luck in life and therefore for his rages; that if she will prove that she loves him by treating him nicer and being more docile and obedient, he will change; that if she leaves, he will take the children away from her; that if she leaves, he will kill himself; that if she leaves, he will kill her.

The wife, by this time in men's history having been almost genetically bred to be emotionally and mentally subservient to men, finds this view of herself and of her situation all too reasonable. She has deeply internalized this propaganda, is profoundly brainwashed to believe it all. So she placates, praises, pleads, and grovels. And denies the dangerousness of her situation.

Her husband is cunning enough to intersperse his abuse with a reward or sop just often enough to reinforce her subservient behavior and keep her hopeful that he really *can*, that he really *will*, change. Though the reward

---

[2] From the Power and Control Wheel produced by the Domestic Abuse Intervention Project, 206 West Fourth Street, Duluth, MN, 55806, (218) 722-4134.

is minute—he won't beat her tonight though she deserves it for letting the baby keep him awake—in her deprived condition it appears merciful and kind and evidence that she is behaving correctly, that, small reform by small reform, she can ultimately transform the whole relationship. She confides to the woman next door in a guilty moment that she can see some positive changes—after he beat her last time, for instance, he felt so bad that he gave her permission to take the car the next day to go see her mother.

As grim as this is, it is only a surface picture. On a deeper level, her husband's terrorism interspersed with shows of repentance and humanity are forging a truly sinister bond—intense, wildly paradoxical, and adamant. Some understanding of why women under terror merge so completely with their torturers and so strongly resist awareness of men's perfidy and gynecidal intent helps explain why women as a class the world over bond with and support men's woman-hating, woman-destroying governments, institutions, values, ideologies, and cosmologies. Why, in short, we vote, go to church, believe in male gods, follow male gurus and channeled entities, attend and teach at universities, send our children to school, become lawyers and corporation servers, marry, and work for male-defined "women's rights."

I have found particular clarification of our baffling behavior in the ongoing work of Dee L. R. Graham, Edna Rawlings, and Nelly Rimini, faculty in the Psychology Department at the University of Cincinnati. Their thesis is that we can expand our understanding of SHATTER, as well as the psychological reactions of battered women, by looking at a model called the Stockholm Syndrome.

The Stockholm Syndrome is a construct developed to explain the strong emotional bonding of hostages and prisoners of war to their captors, and by feminist extension, of battered women to their terrorists. In *Loving to Survive*,[3] the authors cite four conditions necessary for this syndrome to develop: first (in the case of a battered woman), she must perceive the terrorist as having powers of life and death over her; second, she must believe that she cannot escape, that her life therefore depends on her captor; third, she must be isolated from outsiders so that his perspective is the only perspective available; and, fourth, she must feel as if her captor has shown her some kindness.[4]

When these conditions are met, she suffers what the authors term "traumatic psychological infantilism," a condition that "causes the victim to cling to the very person who is endangering her life."[5] In addition, the victim's recognition that her abuser holds the power of life and death over her, coupled with the awareness that he has—magnanimously it seems to her—allowed her to

---

[3] Dee L.R. Graham, Edna Rawlings, and Nelly Rimini, *Loving to Survive: Battered Women, Hostages, and the Stockholm Syndrome*, a work in progress, Cincinnati, OH, p. 89. Some of this material has been published in K. Yllo and M. Bograd (Eds.), *Feminist Perspectives on Wife Abuse*. Sage: Beverly Hills, CA, 1988.

[4] Dee L.R. Graham, et al., *Loving to Survive*, p. 3.

[5] Dee L.R. Graham, et al., *Loving to Survive*, p. 4.

live, causes her to cleave to him in what is known as "traumatic bonding": she begins to view him as a "good guy," denying to herself (and others) how dangerous he is,[6] and opposing rescue.[7] In the Women's Movement, we call this phenomenon "seasoning."

Seasoning, traumatic bonding, is incredibly strong. For it to take place, there must be not only a great imbalance in power but also "intermittent violence alternating with warm, friendly, kind behavior."[8] When this happens, and in the absence of other supportive relationships, the victim bonds to the supportive, positive aspect of her abuser.[9] (This helps explain why children of abusive parents often feel strong loyalties to them and do not wish to be separated.) A significant part of this bond (and of her bondage) is that she internalizes his world view,[10] sides with, and identifies with him—and imitates him.

All women in patriarchy are long-term prisoners of war, perpetual hostages. Though we are no doubt in various stages of recovery, we are held fast in the Stockholm Syndrome. In this country, for instance, we have been more successfully isolated from one another

---

[6] Dee L.R. Graham, et al., *Loving to Survive*, p. 5.

[7] Dee L.R. Graham, et al., *Loving to Survive*, p. 2.

[8] Dee L.R. Graham, et al., *Loving to Survive*, p. 6

[9] Dee L.R. Graham, et al., *Loving to Survive*, p. 6.

[10] Dee L.R. Graham, et al., *Loving to Survive*, p. 4.

than in any other—one woman to one individual guard and cell in the suburban nuclear family; our access to public space and to the outside world during one half of every day is limited and controlled by threat of rape; we are economically harassed and deprived—kept from getting decent jobs, made to plead for money from our husband the state, forced to accept an allowance from him; we are forced into prostitution and the sex industry, our sexuality used to sell everything under the sun; we are ground to dust by the courts, by religion, by industry, by schools, by art, by the very form and structure of the system, by every nail in its boot. And of course the shock troops daily hunt us down to torture and murder us.

But underlying this picture that feminists have been calling into visibility for about 200 years is the still-hidden and steely bond forged by the system's life-and-death hold over us, by our perceiving no escape from it, our isolation from any alternative perspective or possibility, and our husband the state's maleficent, utterly designed, intermittent shows of "kindness"—*Roe v. Wade*, for instance.

Women, in our marriage with the patriarchal state, present the classic features of traumatic psychological infantilism and of traumatic bonding. Our basic acceptance of male "reality" and of the necessity of our interacting with it every day is strongest proof that we have incorporated our torturing husband's world view. We believe his lies that we are incompetent and must therefore accept the world pretty much the way he has made it; that we cannot survive economically without him (whereas, in this slave culture, it is *he* who is economically dependent upon *us*); that he is basically a "good guy," the best we can get and we are lucky to have him; that he is the only one who can change our status; that we don't need to leave him because if we placate him, are docile, get permission, we can change him, and tiny reform by tiny reform we can build a happy marriage. We have evidence that our way of dealing with him is effective: after all, he's letting a handful of us do some of the high-status, low-integrity jobs men have always done.[11]

I have heard women involved in male politics say about our political system almost the same words I have heard battered women use about their abusers: "Of course our government isn't perfect, but where is there a better one? With all its faults, it is still the best system [husband] in the world." Like a battered wife, they never think to ask the really relevant question: who said we needed a husband, or a husband-state, *at all*?

In terror that our husband the state will kill us or starve us if we try to leave, many feminists are resisting even the possibility of such a divorce and in classic terror-bonded behavior, are attacking those of us who urge it. But it is clear to me that, having bonded with monsters and their monstrous extension the system—ironically, for what we perceived as "safety"—we are clinging to a

---

[11] So that we won't ask ourselves such questions as: Do we enjoy these kinds of work? Do these jobs really need doing? Upon what values should we decide what work is necessary and useful? What is the most humane way of approaching any given task?

marriage that is lethal to women and to all life.

Though we have so far followed the same pattern in the macrocosm as in the microcosm of patriarchy, there is great hope. After all, every day women free themselves of terrorist husbands. We understand something of what has to happen for them to be able to do this.

Though every woman's experience is unique in many ways, there is a common denominator to them all: she changes how she perceives herself, how she feels about herself, in that relationship. She sets about her internal revolution, deprograms herself, and in the process breaks her dependency upon men's kindness. Whereas once she felt worthless and not deserving of better treatment, something spurs her to begin caring about herself and, most significantly of all, to begin putting herself *first*.

Though that "something" is different with every woman, the results are similar. I remember Helen's story. Helen is a well-educated woman who, in an extremely abusive relationship with Fred for 13 years, displayed all the evidences of terror-bonding. One night she was in the emergency room at the local hospital again. As the doctors were putting her eyeball back into its socket, setting her broken shoulder, and sewing up the knife wounds all over her body, one of them who knew her well by this time said, "You know, Helen, the next time they bring you in here, I'm afraid we'll just have to tell them to wheel you right on through to the morgue."

Suddenly, a crack appeared in the heretofore solid wall of her brainwashing. Through it she saw clearly for the first time that though Fred had always threatened to kill her if she left him, the truth was that he would kill her if she *stayed*. She awoke to her danger, and whereas before she had been afraid of leaving, now she began to feel far more afraid of *not* leaving. She realized that she wanted to live, that she wanted to be happy, that she didn't deserve this. She began to value her own life. Once she began to change significantly how she felt about herself everything else followed.

Before her feelings about herself underwent transformation, asking herself "What shall I *do*?" was a useless exercise. Since she could not imagine herself doing other than she was doing, since she could not extrapolate a new reality in which she felt free as she stood in the middle of the old one in which she felt trapped, she could not imagine what behavior would get her from bondage to liberty. All she could answer when she asked herself "What shall I *do*?" was the same old conditioned answers: be nicer to him, try harder, show him you love him.

What changed everything is that she saw and felt different, and from these different perceptions and feelings, she *became* different. From her new feelings—present even nascently—of worthiness and lovableness began to come behavior she could never have predicted, never have imagined of herself, certainly never could have planned since she had never seen herself act self-respecting, self-loving, or worthy. There is no way she could have known what she would do if she felt that way before she actually watched herself doing it.

An important part of the "everything else" that

followed from or accompanied Helen's revolution was that she deprogrammed herself of her husband's lies, particularly those he told her about herself. She began to question all the assumptions that underlay her behavior, realized that they were all bogus, and that she had learned them from him. After his lies about *her*, for instance, his biggest lies had been about what would make *him* change and consequently what would change the marriage; she saw that he not only didn't change for the better but actively got worse when she behaved as he told her to. Her growing self-love and trust enabled her to push aside the scrims of deception with which he had shrouded their relationship and to begin to see it for what it really was.

One of Helen's biggest revelations was that she couldn't change Fred, that she couldn't change anyone but herself. As soon as the fact took up firm residence in her emotional repertoire that she had no moral obligation even to *try* to change him, that she had no moral obligation to him at all, only a deep obligation to herself, she left the marriage.

What happens to women like Helen individually in their marriages is happening globally among women as a group. It is called the Women's Liberation Movement and its enunciation is feminism. But whereas many women have left their microcosmic husbands and all their rules and demands, as a group we have yet to leave the partner of our macrocosmic marriage bed—the patriarchal state—and its imperatives, imperatives that are identical with those of its extensions and servants, the Freds of the world.

What is our primary fear when we entertain the idea of leaving our husband the state? That he will kill us and destroy everything. Though the truth is, as it was with Helen and Fred, that he will kill us and destroy everything *if we stay*, like the battered women we are, we believe deeply that our presence, our pleading and begging, is what is keeping him from his ultimate destructiveness. Our conviction that if we stop fearing and monitoring him, he will go berserk, is such nonsense that it is clearly a deliberate part of our terror-based programming. He has gone berserk anyway. With our eyes pinned to his lapels day and night for thousands of years he has grown increasingly lunatic. With our eyes riveted upon him he has been killing us and the world around us since the day god became male. The evidence is that our behavior and our emotional and economic support has facilitated our monster husband the patriarchal state in all his manifestations throughout history.

I mention economic support because one of women's most frequent objections to my suggestion that we stop resisting Fred the Fed and divorce him at once is that we must stay in order to stop him from building more, and more lethal, bombs. At this point, I remind my terrified sisters of the United Nations' statistic that confirms our slavery: women do two-thirds of the world's work, make one-tenth of the world's money, and own less than one-hundredth of the world's property. If we are doing most of the work and men are making nine-tenths of the money, it means that women are men's resources, that we are men's wealth—as the slaves' bodies and energy and labor and creativity and loyalty and emotional richness and culture are always the source of the master's wealth. Therefore our presence in patriarchy is absolutely necessary in order for men to have the wherewithal to do their war work, day by day. Our presence in this marriage makes possible men's bombs and tanks and guns and bullets and planes and ships. Our leaving this marriage, taking ourselves and all our abundance away from Fed Fred, is the fastest and surest way to stop his production of death machines.

There are other economic considerations, women re-mind me. When Helen leaves Fred, chances are pretty good that she will plummet into poverty. This, they say, frightens women most, and I believe them. For this reason, whatever we do now must have as its foremost necessity establishing a firm, independent, economic base for women, and we are beginning to see how this might be done.[12]

I also remember that in the midst of terror, battered women cannot see their alternatives, though outsiders can. I think the same is true for women in patriarchy. In the midst of it, we think there are no alternatives. But if we could stand outside it for only a moment, we would see that we have many options. A handy measure in my life is that when I am *sure* there are no alternatives, I can be absolutely certain that I am listening to my conditioning. Regardless of how circumscribed the situation seems to

---

[12] This is the subject of the last section of this book.

be, there are *always* choices.

If we want to know what will happen when women leave our husband the state, all we need to do is look at what happened when Helen left Fred. Nothing burst into flames; there was simply no marriage where one had been before. We can look high and low for Fred's ugly, vicious regime, his unjust, humiliating system of rules for that family, his institutions and traditions, but they are nowhere to be found. It takes two for sadism to exist.[13] Fred's and Helen's marriage required Helen; it simply ceased to exist when she left, and is gone forever.

Andra Medea, internationally known expert on conflict, discovered this phenomenon through her comparative study of street and business fighting. In describing it, she concludes that in "dominance-oriented conflict"— conflict in which the aim of the attacker is to dominate the victim—interaction forms the key link. The attacker *must* have a response from the victim in order to go on; in fact, the attacker *craves* a response because the response solidifies his control.[14] A button I bought in the Crazy Ladies Bookstore in Cincinnati sums it up: "Power means

---

[13] Though I acknowledge a Victim mode as one of women's programmed roles, I no longer speak of masochism at all. I am tired of men's self-serving analysis that women are in abusive relationships because we are masochistic by nature and want to be hurt. What they call masochism is a condition that could more accurately be called "frozen fright," "a hysterical, dissociative phenomenon characterized by numbness, or paralysis of affect" caused by perpetual terror (Dee L.R. Graham, et al., *Loving to Survive*, p. 4.)

[14] Andra Medea, "Medea's Laws of Conflict," p. 9.

73

not having to respond." [15]

"This sort of attacker can put on a tremendous display of power," Medea continues, "which is often no more than a mask for fundamental weakness. We see it all the time with abusive husbands: the awesome show of power hiding a basic fear and weakness. . . The abusive husband deeply needs the wife, the wife can typically do without the abusive husband." [16]

Medea also makes the point strongly that "the very nature of dominance-oriented attacks is to twist reality." [17]

When women leave patriarchy—when we untwist reality and realize that we do not have to respond to this system, just as the abused wife one day stops believing she has to work with her batterer or within the parameters he has set down and stops responding—patriarchy will simply cease to exist. It won't go up in smoke; it will disappear. It takes two groups to do tyranny: the tyrants and the slaves. Tyrants never stop doing tyranny until the slaves stop responding in the necessary way for tyranny to be done to them. When they stop, the game is up.

---

[15] Ayofemi Stowe, in a performance piece called "Talking About Talking, the Power to Shape the World" that she wrote and performed with Robin Podolsky in 1987, also says something about the necessity of response to power: "When I was in Africa, I learned about the concept of Muntu. It says that every time you call a tree a tree, you reaffirm the power of that tree, the existence of the tree. I wonder if refusing to talk about the tree somehow diminishes the tree" (p. 12A).

[16] Andra Medea, "Medea's Laws of Conflict," p. 5.

[17] Andra Medea, "Medea's Laws of Conflict," p. 11.

I've been divorced twice in my life: once by a husband and once by a church. Before those divorces, I couldn't imagine what I'd do, how I'd live, without a husband, without a church. I couldn't believe that there were genuine alternatives. I was afraid of such enormous changes, afraid of trying to find a new nonconventional, nontraditional path, afraid of the pain of separation.

But in neither case did the pain last long, and I slipped so easily and with such growing joy into other modes of thinking and being that now I am no longer the least afraid of divorce. This is fortunate since I am well along in my process of divorcing the abusive husband all women have in common, the patriarchal state. Gleefully and gladly I am throwing him out of my home, out of my bed, out of my mind, out of my heart—out of my life. As I deprogram myself of his lies, I see him as the weak fearful drunken blusterer he is, and I am not afraid of him anymore.

Leaving our abusive husband-state seems risky to many women. It is hard to overcome the terror-produced belief that we are responsible for men's behavior and that if we stop being responsible, instant catastrophe will ensue. But since our best efforts to change them have only spurred them on, like Helen and all other battered women we have nothing to lose and everything to gain by simply walking out of this marriage, divorcing Fred the Fed, and with our sisters creating the world we want right now.

I have come to the place in my spiritual development where anything less than this bores me unutterably.

Recently a TV reporter asked me on a live news program what I thought of the 1988 Presidential candidates. I answered, "Oh, are they having another election? I don't know who's running but I *do* know what they're saying. I could write all their speeches myself—if I could keep awake long enough."

"But you can't deny," he protested, "that whoever is elected will have power to affect your life."

"Oh, but you're wrong. I can and do deny that those men have power," I countered. Though I hadn't time to explain it to him then, coming to that point in my thinking was a crucial step for me. It seems to me a step that any woman might take who is intent upon living in a new world now.

Part II

CHALLENGING OUR ASSUMPTIONS

Preface to Part II

B ecause our freedom depends on it, deprogramming ourselves from patriarchy's brainwashing is the single most crucial task before us. It is also the most difficult. To do it, we who have been a domesticated species for thousands of years must recover our wild minds, our thoroughly skeptical and irreverent facilities. We must ask ourselves at least a dozen times a day such questions as: Who said so? Who benefits from my thinking this? How does this thought or feeling keep me patriarchy's chattel? How has this idea kept the Women's Movement securely in men's hands?

Asking myself that last question, for instance, enabled me some time ago to understand how the media determines the direction of our Movement. All day long the trumpets of patriarchy blare in our ears from every direction that the Women's Movement is about "ishoos"—"women's ishoos." (You have to squinch your mouth into a tiny "o" to say "ishoos.") Although every so often women get the feeling that the Women's Movement is about something distinctly other than this, something immense and beautiful, the media's constant delineation of it as "ishoos" soon sets them straight again: what women *really* want is equal pay and child care.

In this way patriarchy—particularly its media—has defined our Movement for us from the beginning. In this way we have been persuaded to pay attention to the things that would make least change in the status quo, concentrate our energies on areas that could not be seriously restructured until more basic shifts in values were made. Equal pay for equal work, for example, is a true impossibility in an exchange system; child care can never be restructured satisfactorily for mothers in patriarchy. Our focus on the red herring of "ishoos" has caused us to see ourselves small and blurry in a small and blurry Movement, like a bad snapshot taken from a distance.

For years I have known that everything that men have told us is true is in fact false, if not in an obvious then in a devious, sneaky way, like "ishoos." Nevertheless, recognizing any of the hundreds of implanted and false assumptions underlying everything I think and do every day has been the hardest labor of my life.

In Part II, I offer some of the insights I have gathered as I have tried to question every aspect of my heretofore automatic belief system. It is irrelevant to me whether they are "right" or "wrong." What *is* important is that they give me another perspective, they broaden the possibilities, they encourage wildness and creativity in me. These—the untamed, inspired mind and will—are what I value. The *habit* of not accepting anything out of an unexamined faith in someone else's world view—this is what I cherish.

As each of us tells the others the foolishness we have ferreted out of our own minds, we encourage this habit in our species. This Part is intended as a contribution to women's quick recovery of the habit of wild, inventive thought and action.

CHAPTER 4

The Women in Power
And Other News

Trying to explain to reporters in 30 seconds or fewer why I no longer believe men have power is, of course, impossible. Even if I were to spend hours explaining why men's *defining* power and their defining it as *external* together expose a mammoth deception, they would not take me seriously. As far as they are concerned, men's having the power on our world is a cultural given, and to suggest otherwise is to indulge in semantic hocus-pocus.

But the feminist process of discovering in ourselves, and of disentangling from, every venerable premise of global male culture is unlike any other emancipation, and sometimes does resemble magic. Looking back into time as far as we can see, we find no evidence of any people who had to start from scratch in establishing a new world mind as women are now having to do. We may not always know what to do to bring this world into being, but we have been getting a clearer idea all the time of what is not useful, of what *not* to do.

Scrutinizing language has been part of this effort from the first. When we deal with language, we engage with symbol, the strongest magic. Feminists understand that one of the subterfuges by which men came to own the world was by appropriating language, embedding messages in it that justified their tyranny and by doing so, literally changing the face of reality. Although we try to be exceedingly cautious and on guard as we use their languages, they are so studded with word-mines that with every thought we think, internal explosions threaten our tenuous new reality, our tender budding self-love. If we are not careful, we find ourselves assuming that language's sly, subliminal memos report the one and only possible way to see the world. We then not only believe those messages but act on them.

Such a classified memo is the word "power," another concept about which men have set the limits of feminist debate. We often end up trying to make distinctions between "power-over"—which we perceive as masculinist—and "power-with" or "power-to"—to women a tamer form of the unruly concept. But what we have rarely done is ask ourselves why we accepted any part of men's definition of power in the first place.

Power is a confusing concept only if we assume that men have defined it disinterestedly—a pernicious assumption advocated by the guys who brought us a system founded on lies.

I often hear feminists speak of "the men in power," and until recently used that phrase often myself. But one day as I went to say it, it stuck in my throat.

"Who says men have power?" a voice inside me demanded.

"Why, *they* say so," I answered.

"Who benefits from the belief that what men say is power *is* power?" the voice insisted.

"*They* benefit, of course," I said.

"What an extraordinary coincidence," the voice mused.

Such a suspicious coincidence, in fact, that it turned my thinking in quite another direction.

Underlying all my deprogramming myself of patriarchal dogma is the assumption that *nothing* men have said is true—at least in the way they said it was; that their view of reality, past and present, is relentlessly warped and twisted and, most often, just flat-out wrong. Not understanding the basic principles of life and love that underlie everything, they cannot be assumed to have understood anything.

Thinking this over, I realized that since men own the language and can name their hanky-panky whatever they wish, obviously they have always tried to name it something highly politic, something with terrific propaganda force. When they cunningly chose "power," we believed them. Then, looking at the behavior they called powerful and noticing right away that *we* didn't act like that, we concluded that we were powerless. Consequently, we *felt* powerless.

But men's insistence that they have power is not only classic patriarchal reversal but also wishful thinking. They are experts at creating a reality by "acting as if." Contrary to their propaganda and to the common belief it produced, men do *not* have power. Patriarchy is a philosophy and a regime of infinite weakness.

The only way men could ever have been regarded as powerful is by doing what they did—stealing the language and naming weakness "power," defining power as ownership and control of others, as the holding of slaves by incalculable violence and terrorism, as the willingness to destroy life.

Patriarchy's basis in violence and death is proof of its weakness, if any is needed. Violence is the offspring of weakness, spawned by emotional neediness, feelings of insecurity and powerlessness, worthlessness and fear. It is an indication not of strength of character but rather of a fateful characterological defectiveness. Because of its weakness, patriarchy is now dying in its infancy, a mere 5,000 years old and some say even younger. In contrast, women's culture flourished for at least 200,000 years.

Patriarchy is weak and nongenerative because it is reactionary through and through. Arising from opposition to women's world, it sprang from profoundly negative impulses, from motives of hatred and revenge, from a lust to destroy all that was womanly and creative of life, all, that is, that was powerful. It continues on this bent. Corruption cannot beget power.

Power is the generative, positive stuff of life, and because integrity is its source, it cannot destroy or hurt or limit or debase. Power is what women have and always have had. We have always been the generative, positive people on this planet, which is why men have had to redefine and obfuscate the true nature of power.

Since genuine power stems from integrity and can exist only in the presence of integrity, women cannot possibly have power in men's misogynist system (and of course men, being misogynist, cannot have power either). Engagement with the system is for women a profound betrayal of self.

I look out upon the world men have made—their legislatures, courts, churches, schools, art, architecture, their politics, their economics—and I don't see anything I would have done as they have done it. *Not one single thing.* Their system does not reflect me at all, neither my mode of being in the world nor my world view; rather, it is inimical to all I love, all I desire, all I *am*. Its every aspect pains me to look at, to think about; it hurts me on all levels of my life; it is not my home.

To me this means that in reality I am excluded from patriarchy not by the fact of men's control but by my own women's values, my own perspectives, my own female way of being human in the world. These values, these perspectives, these ways make patriarchy alien to me and to all women, put us psychically, emotionally, and spiritually outside their system.

Outside their system, then, is where we genuinely live and have our being; any other notion is pure illusion.

Since we can only be authentic, wholly and truly ourselves outside their system, only outside can we have
integrity—and, therefore, power.

This is perhaps the most important feminist fact I
know, that integrity is the source of all power, that power
comes from loyalty to one's best self. We cannot have
power in men's system because we cannot be true to our
best selves there. We cannot have power in men's system
because in order to be in it at all we must be like
them—think like them, act like them, be junior men. In
a win/lose paradigm, a dominance-oriented conflict, such
as patriarchy, "whoever imitates, loses." [1]

Because women can never really be part of the Old
Boys' Club no matter what positions they hold, what their
presence in systemic structures does is to provide for
other women a model of powerlessness and betrayal of
self. Their presence there says that the best way to be a
woman is to try to be a man, to deny that we are different,
to be too cowardly to say, "All this is purest humbug!"
Their imitative behavior shouts the message that men's
world view and their ways are not only okay but prefer-
able. Because their torture-induced need for approval
from men and their system is greater than the need for
approval from themselves, they model slavery to their
sisters. They are deeply dependent, deeply servile in
ways that their superficial "liberation" masks.

But simply by being female, we are, whether we are

---

[1] Andra Medea, "Medea's Laws of Conflict," p. 4.

aware of it or not, in the truest sense outside their system at any given moment, and therefore can have incredible power *right now*. All we need do is understand and believe that this is true and not be afraid to *take* our power.

And stop renouncing it in favor of male control, which is exactly what we do. I learned the logistics of this control give-away in the microcosm of my own patriarchal home,[2] in my own kitchen.

Several years ago, when my third child was 17, he and I had a typical parent-teenager clash in the kitchen one night, one of a great many throughout his adolescence, this time about drugs. He stormed downstairs to his room and slammed the door, leaving me standing in the middle of the room feeling wretched and powerless.

Even having already reared two adolescents, I had no more idea how to get the present one to do what he should than I had had with the first two. The task seemed impossible. I had lived in terror for years—terror that they would be unhappy, that they would do drugs, that they would self-destruct—and doing everything I could think of to prevent these disasters had neither lessened the terror nor changed their behavior. Although the first two had made it through somehow, I wasn't at all sure if or how my actions had helped or hindered those outcomes, and the trial-and-error of it had nearly undone me. I couldn't imagine, standing there that night, how I was

---

[2] All homes are patriarchal until we get patriarchy out of our minds and souls.

going to live through two more adolescents.

Suddenly, I began to feel very angry—in my experience always a first sign of returning health. I realized that I was furious at the anguish I had suffered so long as a mother and the misery that seemed still to stretch so endlessly before me. I felt as if I couldn't wait to be happy until all my kids were over 30 and safe (besides, mothers of over-30s had told me that their kids were still never safe); I'd been the best mother I'd known how to be for over 20 years, and I deserved to be happy. What's more, I deserved it *now*! I was nearly 50 years old. When had I thought I was going to begin?

Then, thinking of my tyrant son sulking down in his room, and feeling an unaccustomed invulnerability, a new firmness at the center, I thought, "That kid can go to hell in a handbasket! I would be sorry, because I love him and I don't intend to stop loving him. And I'll do what I can to prevent it—but not like before. I can't live his life for him; I can't make him do what I want him to do. He's just going to have to decide for himself whether he's going to self-destruct or not, and I'm going to have to be happy no matter what he decides."

I felt as if I had been holding his heel as he hung upside down over the abyss. One cannot live one's own life while holding someone else's heel. I decided I needed to love myself first and be true to myself, do what was best for me, assuming that whatever is best for me is best for everyone around me.

Though I didn't understand for a long time the scope of my change that night, and though I still had much work to do to make that change permanent, looking back what is clear is that I was finally beginning to understand the dynamics of how women give our power to men. I was getting hold of a basic principle of power, that when we make our feelings of well-being or security or safety dependent upon someone else's behavior, we hand them the opportunity, even the invitation, to destroy us.

I realized that night that I would never have control of my life if I continued to make my internal climate contingent upon whether or not my children or anyone else outside me did what I wanted them to do. As long as I did, I would live in perpetual terror that they would not take care of my feelings. I would always be trying to change *them* so they would act in a way that would make *me* feel secure and happy. It had become unmistakably clear in that flash that because I couldn't control anyone or change anyone but myself, it was emotional suicide to put the responsibility for my happiness in someone else's hands.

In some inchoate way that night, I knew that I had to hold *all* the responsibility for my feelings in my own hands or I would never be safe or free, that otherwise I would always be manipulatable, out of my own control, always at someone else's mercy. Since no one can care about me as much as I care about myself, I would always get hurt, sometimes very badly. If I continued in this vulnerable, powerless mode, having four children would mean staying hooked up to four conduits to agony for the rest of my life. I felt as if I would die if I continued in the old way.

Without knowing exactly what I was doing, but for the sake of survival, I detached myself from my children then as sources of well-being for me, took the responsibility away from them, where I couldn't control it, back into myself where it belonged. At the same time I realized, momentarily at least, that I was not responsible for any other person's well-being or security or safety either;[3] that there comes a time when we must each learn to put our own lives first, realize that no one else can or will or should consistently bear the burden of making us feel safe and loved, and find our source of satisfaction and safety *within ourselves.* In any other thinking, disaster looms.

That night in my kitchen these ideas were largely still feelings—strong, internalized feelings of love for myself and a dedication to my own happiness, the basis of integrity. With these feelings full upon me, without thinking of a plan, without asking "What shall I *do*?" I went down and confronted my son. I have no idea what I said; there is a limited repertoire in such situations. Certainly I didn't say or do anything I hadn't said or done a dozen times before. I couldn't have put into words the change I'd just gone through enough to articulate it to myself let alone to him.

The difference was in how I *was.* The instant he reluctantly opened his door to me, he knew the old game was over. He knew he was standing in the presence of New Mom, mom who could not be manipulated or

---

[3] Anyone over the age of 16, that is.

bullied, a woman in her power. Regardless of what his ears were picking up, all his antennae were quivering with the message that had become a part of my being, of my aura: I had let go of his heel. He knew without conscious thought that whether or not he plunged to his death in the abyss below or decided to change his course was now entirely up to him. I was handing him back the responsibility for his life.

Overnight—and I do not mean that metaphorically; I mean literally overnight, between the night of October 16 and the morning of October 17—the chronic disquiet in our home disappeared. My son's life changed dramatically in the direction I had been trying to get it to change for years, and it has stayed changed. Of course, he could have chosen to self-destruct, though most people, given the responsibility and the choice, do not. But even if he had made that choice, I would have been all right. I would have grieved terribly, but my heart's fire would not have been extinguished with guilt as it would once have been. Grief softens and dims with time, but guilt is eternally sharp and glittery bright. (A part of us does not survive the guilt patriarchy reserves for mothers.)

When women make our well-being, our feelings of security and safety, dependent upon whether or not the system is amenable to us, whether or not the men who control this world behave as we believe they must for us to be "all right"—if they stop building bombs, if congress passes the right bills, if Bork is kept off the Supreme Court; in short, if we think we can't be happy until the men change, we invite them to hurt us, give them control over our innermost reality, put the responsibility for our lives in their weak, violent hands. When we make our internal state contingent upon their behavior—behavior we can neither control nor change—we give up all chance for independence and freedom, and ultimately, we give up all chance for life. Because we are the only ones we can change and control, we must depend upon ourselves for freedom. We must use our mighty power now to create a home for ourselves and all other living things.

Someone is sure to say at this juncture, "Well, that's pretty rhetoric, but if men don't have power, why can they still rape us, still beat us, still impoverish us? Call it what you will, it looks like power to me!"

Alix Dobkin, Susan Horwitz, and I were talking one afternoon at Wiminfest in Albuquerque. Alix had recently returned from Australia and New Zealand, and was still intoxicated with the women she'd met and the stories she'd heard there. Three of the stories were about authentic power, women's power, the power that comes from within.

In a small frontier town in Australia there is a group of women who meet often to be together and do womanly things. Though they never announce publicly when or where they will meet, a group of dangerous red-necks in the town frequently discover this information—perhaps they sense it in their threatened gonads—and arrive on the scene to harass them, *seriously* harass them.

One night as they were meeting, the women heard the men pull up in a pick-up outside, spill out, and come clanking with their spurs and guns, all liquored up, their talk vulgar and boisterous, into the building. When the men entered the room where the women were, they found the women sitting on the floor each with her eyes locked into the woman's eyes opposite her in the circle, silently and deeply looking into another woman's eyes, totally focused on one another.

The men, who expected to be met with terror and pleading, couldn't get their bearings. They milled about with much bravado for awhile, but as the women's focus held, they grew quieter and finally shuffled out, got in the pick-up, and drove away.

This is power.

Another night when the women were meeting, the men came again and parked themselves outside the door, shooting off their guns, brandishing big sticks, trying to terrorize the women as they waited for them to come out. Which the women did—in single file, humming. Such refusal to be afraid, such certainty of their own power, such centeredness, totally befuddled the mob, and they parted and let the women through.

This is power.

On another evening, the men came and left, promising to return. So each woman sat and envisioned how she wanted the evening to go. One of the members of the group arrived late, explaining that she had had difficulty getting around the men's pick-up, which had overturned down the road!

This is power, and it comes from within, from how we feel about ourselves, from believing that we are powerful and that anyone who has to control others by violence is weak and fearful and simply no match for us. Power comes from not viewing ourselves as vulnerable, as victims, as at men's mercy. When enough of us access this power within ourselves, no woman, even the most terrorized, will be rapable, beatable, assaultable, or impoverishable.

Men call this "magical thinking" in an attempt to discredit it. Anything that men want to discredit interests me enormously. Why would they bother to notice it or to name it at all, to say nothing of going out of their way to pour calumny upon it, if it were simply harmless and stupid? Who does it benefit for recognition of a different mode of being in the world to be written off as "magical thinking?" If all people realized the extent of their personal power, no one could control anyone else. I believe it is a natural law that power—to create and to protect creation—springs from within, from our beliefs and feelings. Men have had to blind and deafen and numb us to our immense powers in order to keep us under control. Surely this is the way they took over the world. Let us be advised.

Some soul, desperate to preserve the old belief and feeling, as we have all been taught to do, might say at this point, "You may not believe men have power, but women can't have babies without them, and this is a definite power men have over women."

I'm so glad that this imaginary desperate soul brought that up. It reminds me of another story Alix told us that day in Albuquerque. She said that one of the aboriginal cultures in Australia is reputed to be the oldest living society in the world. In that community, women are greatly respected and very influential. They have many of their own rituals, rituals it is literally unthinkable that the men could intrude upon. In the myth of this group, and basic to the women's feelings about themselves, basic to their power, is a story of the long time, the ages and ages, when only women lived on this earth. Obviously, these people have no illusions about the necessity of men to the continuation of the species.

"But," my hypothetical desperate soul may say, "even if the story is true—and it can't be—that was *then*. Parthenogenesis doesn't happen these days."

But maybe it does. Ruth Barrett told me at the National Women's Music Festival in Bloomington in June 1988 that doctors admit that about one in every 10,000 births is parthenogenic, and if doctors give a number on such a subject, we know it has to be a low estimate. Earlier that week a woman in Albuquerque told me that a great deal of research had been done on the subject at Berkeley in the 60s and 70s and that it was either forced to go underground or has been destroyed. I have asked Ruth to let me know if she ever runs into a woman who claims to be pregnant by parthenogenesis or to have given birth to a child so conceived.

Since true power moves from the inside out, parthenogenesis makes soundest sense.

As more and more women find our power and experiment with living in it, however, we would do well to remember how frightened oppressed people become when some of their group break through to freedom, how well-trained all women have been to clamp the fetters around the ankles of any of our kind who give signs of escaping. If we remember that women have been prisoners of war for millennia, we will be more understanding and forgiving of one another when, in our terror-bond with patriarchy, we try to destroy one another.

At the same time, of course, we must not let anyone's fear of our power make us also afraid of it or distract us from practicing how to live in it more fully every day. We would be wise to remember that sometimes when women are in their own power, acting with the authority that comes from within—an alien mode in patriarchy and one that enrages some other women (a rage that I believe stems from terror)—they are denounced as demagogues and told that they are leading women astray.

The positive side of such behavior is that it gives us important information about the denouncers. First, it tells us that the frightened ones are tempted *themselves* by the ideas and world view and mode of power of the women they fear, that *they* are tempted to divorce their most cherished beliefs, the ones from which they get greatest reward—their view of themselves as victims, for instance, or as "partners" of men—and are terrified by these feelings of disloyalty to their captors. Second, it tells us that they fear that all women who come within the strong women's ken will be similarly tempted and may succumb, in which case the torturers will kill them all. Third, it says that because they do not trust themselves, they do not trust other women; otherwise they would not view women as unthinking sheep who can be led any which way by women who dare be their fully powerful selves. Fourth, it exposes their fear of women's being powerful in one another's presence, the fear that we can neither withstand nor cope with genuine power, only with control, and it says that they are afraid of their own power. Fifth, it reveals that they do not love themselves because if they did, they would not be threatened by women's diversity and could stop trying to control women, could let them each be who and where they are in their journeys whether they agree with them or not.

Any woman who other women are trying to pull out of her power through the widening cracks in her programming back again into men's dead world must of course simply continue on her course, growing in her ability to access and live in her power moment by moment. None of us needs worry about leading other women into error. Women are neither stupid nor sheep, and certainly will not follow other women blindly. We can all be trusted to take from one another what we find useful, think over any new possibilities that interest us, and leave the rest.

Being, without compunction, as powerful as we know how to be among one another—in women's way, from within, the way that does not weaken others—each of us gives other women permission to practice being amazing to themselves. But this is incidental. Paramount is the fact that by doing so we fulfill our responsibility to *ourselves*. For example, for my own sake, I always give the most persuasive, most impassioned speeches of which I am capable, letting my power rise and fill me utterly, enjoying myself and the strong women in the audience so much that I haven't room to worry about the extremely unlikely possibility that I will lead any of them astray.

But I do keep a closer watch over my language than I have done before, remembering that words create reality. I know that if I were to say "the men in power," I would give the women hearing me the message that I acceded to that lie, and I would again reinforce my own former illusion that because what *men* have is power, *women* are powerless.

Now when someone wants a comment from me about "the men in power" and their current mischief, I say, "So the men in weakness are setting up another futile meeting in Geneva (or wherever), you say? You say the men in weakness are bombing, raping, torturing, murdering, pillaging, and laying waste? Ho hum. What else is old?"

Then I tell them what's new: "The women in power today are recreating themselves and all society. The women in power today are breaking free of fear of men's weakness, free of the necessity for men's approval and 'kindness,' free of the patriarchal imperative that we must change men, getting them to do for us what must be done, free of the lie that we cannot do it ourselves. The women in power today know not only that the men in weakness cannot change the world, but that it is *women* who are rising in every race, every class, every nation of the world to decide the course of human events, the fate of all life. The women in power today are forming communities around the earth, establishing a new economic base, a new order of plenty and peace. The women in power, in genuine power—that's us, and that's what's new."

CHAPTER 5

Oldspapers and
The Evening Olds

A nd that's *all* that's new. So every time we say the
words "newspapers" and "evening news"—let alone
actually read their pages and watch them on the TV
screen—we fortify the assumption necessary to patriarchy
that men have power, that they are doing something new,
that they are changing things, that the system is dynamic,
alive, fresh, real. Those words reconfirm our fears that
because what feminists are doing is not in the "news," we
are not doing anything new or vital, not making any
difference, that we have no power, that we are not
important.

When we stop to think about it, we know that none
of this is true. We know that, contrary to the promotion
hook in the word "news," patriarchy is obsolete, stagnant,

weak and false.

One glance at what men call newspapers confirms this. There is nothing in them from front to back that we couldn't have predicted. Any one of us, if required, could sit down at a desk and create a most plausible "newspaper" from scratch. Why? Because there is absolutely nothing new in any of them whatever. Patriarchy, like the senile system it is, merely repeats itself endlessly, mumbles the same old formula for success: bigness, control, winning, money, status, fear, hatred, scarcity, violence.

I am not willing deliberately to reinforce my self-hatred by lying to myself with words such as these that I *know* are harmful to me. So when I must, I speak of the *olds*papers and the evening *olds*, keeping my imagistic mind as free of manipulative clutter as possible.

I no longer subscribe to or read oldspapers or olds magazines or watch or listen to the olds on TV or radio. I know that women are the only ones with the power to do anything new in the world, the only creative people now on earth. Women's world is just being born, men's is dead and lies around us rotting, waiting for us to bury and forget it. This is still so hard for me to remember, to internalize, and to *feel* that I take great care not to subvert my delicate new consciousness by slipping comfortably into my former language, laden as it is with false assumptions.

Those who think this is a silly notion need only ask themselves how many women they know have stopped reprogramming themselves with self-hate and powerlessness every day by refusing to read the oldspapers or watch the evening olds; they are the neighbors, friends, kin of those who pooh-pooh such behavior. Everywhere I go I meet such women, some of whom would not dream of calling themselves feminists. But they are women of our time. They are tired of feeling vulnerable and victimized, and they have come to the end of toleration of men's weakness and stupidity parading as power and brilliance. They tell me that it bores them and they don't care how politically incorrect that sounds to others.

Me either.

CHAPTER 6

Just/Us and Hequality[1]

Nor do I care how politically incorrect it sounds to acknowledge how appalled I am that I ever accepted the concept of justice, another example of men's attempt to make us perceive power as external and dichotomous. Though it is symbolized by scales held by a blindfolded figure, in fact objective justice is an oxymoron. Justice is securely based in values, and values by definition are neither blind nor impersonal.

Rather than being some sort of moral absolute, justice was created as a loyal servant to patriarchy, spawning a system dependent upon someone's meting out upon others either reward for conformity to patriarchal values or

---

[1] These are Marlene Mountain's words that she lent me in conversations in January and March 1989.

punishment for flaunting them.[2] The concept of justice cannot exist without acceptance of patriarchy's identification of power with hierarchy and external control.

The assumption that any man or woman, no matter how "good," should or even *can* decide what is best for anyone else without being influenced by personal biases and beliefs, not only dignifies men's absurd belief in pure disembodied logos, but reinforces the idea that it is reasonable, nay "natural," for some to have control over others. And reinforces the absurdity that power automatically attaches to those who control.

In creating the illusion that someone outside us must sit in judgment upon us, justice sanctions and gives life-support to tyranny. Tyranny can survive only so long as most of us believe that power is externally based, that someone else has the right to decide what is "just" for us, what we "deserve." A belief in god and god-surrogates is essential to tyranny.

Inherent in justice is the eye-for-an-eye authorization of retaliation and revenge. One of my most difficult tasks as a mother has been to persuade my children not to be spiteful and mean in response to spite and meanness. This has been made particularly onerous not only by their study of the behavior of famous men in history, but also by watching present famous men rationalize bombing a city because a U.S. ship has been fired upon. With such

---

[2] Having been a mother for over 25 years, I no longer believe in the efficacy of punishment. It has never improved any of my children's behavior for long.

models of moral pathology parading as "justice," women's job of humanizing children has been made well-
nigh impossible.

The concept of justice is based on distrust and hatred
of human nature and is hostile to the development of self-
trust, self-rule, and trust of others. Because it is external
coercion, not self-government, justice is always a weapon
of those in control. It cannot function in behalf of those
controlled; it is not "just" that they should be controlled
in the first place.

Since I do not want justice, what would I propose instead? I want compassion and generosity, first from
myself. If I can understand and love myself, I will be
merciful and loving to others. If enough of us can deal
with ourselves generously and truthfully, kindly, loving-
ly, mercifully, there will be no need for courts, for laws,
for the top-heavy, top-down inherent cruelty of justice. I
am tired of being controlled by others. What I want is
self-rule. I want true anarchy. I am ready for it.

. . . .

Like justice, equality is a word I don't hear very often
any more among the feminists I meet and with whom I
associate. Many of us, having found equality an obfusca-
ting concept, have long since rejected it as a goal. Equal
to whom, we ask? In what way? Equality, like justice an
externally referenced word, must always involve comparison, and as far as I am concerned, being a feminist means
that I stop comparing myself against external standards or
other people—particularly men—taking to heart my

knowledge that because each of us is truly incomparable, the concept of "equality" is profoundly patriarchal. That we judge ourselves with criteria not of our own devising and compare ourselves with others in almost all aspects of our lives is a stunning achievement of the fathers.

In addition, what we *think* of as equality (i.e., when we are not aware of it as a conditional, dualistic concept) is not even a possibility in a hierarchical system. I can't think why I ever thought it *was* any more than I can remember why I once thought it was a desirable end. Men admit that even when two of *them* meet, before they can so much as begin to talk they must both decide which one of them is in the one-up position and which in the one-down, using the criteria first of race, then of wealth and status measured in dozens of ways. Without imposing their hierarchical paradigm upon every experience, men cannot move an inch in any aspect of their lives.

If no *man* ever perceives any other man as an equal but instead always either higher or lower in status than he, where do *women* fit into patriarchy's "equality" ideal? The answer is of course that we neither do nor even *can* fit and that equality therefore is not possible in patriarchy. Further, what we have always mistakenly called "equality" is really HEquality, a construct that bears no resemblance to what men say equality is but instead is a variation on the theme of tyranny.

More than this, however. The concept of equity is only possible to the dualistic mind, the mind that must posit "unequal" in order to posit "equal." When we realize that its existence is dependent upon the existence of inequality—not just in our minds but also in the world—we see that equality is an artifact of dichotomous patriarchal thought.

So in solemnly teaching us to revere and desire equality, men have played a great joke on us. But now that we have caught them out, perhaps we can acknowledge their drollery by referring to this venerable nonideal in the future not only as hequality but also as "hee-heequality."

With what shall we replace this figment, this dream of "equality?" I suggest that it was part of a long and ancient nightmare and that we just let it go. It needs no replacement. Feminist anarchy is simple: self-love resulting in love of others out of which springs behavior in the best interests of everyone. To some that sounds impossible. But it is not nearly so complicated, not nearly so difficult to maintain, as patriarchy, and it is home to the human heart, where it longs to go, where it knows it is *possible* to go, where, guided by the rising of women out of self-hatred and out of our consequent facilitation of men's destructiveness, it is heading at the speed of light.

CHAPTER 7

The Otters of the Universe

I often hear women say something like this: "I came back this time around to learn patience (or forgiveness, or tolerance) because I didn't learn it in my former lives." When I hear this kind of thinking, my alarm bells begin to go off, the bells that peal "Patriarchy! Beware!"

For the fathers, living is never enough in itself. There must be some external purpose for it, some lesson to be learned, some difficult and far-off goal to be attained, something to "win" (always with a measuring, comparative eye on everyone else's progress toward that end). If we succeed, we are rewarded, in this case by being incarnated into greater happiness and a more refined consciousness next time. If we fail, we must come back to try again, to atone for our failure. Patriarchy purposefully trains our eyes upon the future (which never comes), teaching us to live now in such a way that we might live better in the future, trapping us in the pernicious lie that living is a means to some end other than simply being alive in the perfectly satisfying richness of the present.

I recently received a letter from a couple of students doing a study on "the meaning of life," questioning a certain number of us about our perceptions of it. They left a large space for the answer and suggested attaching additional pages if necessary. I sent a postcard on which I wrote one short line, "The meaning of life is to be alive."

The fathers have taught us to view life as a very heavy, serious, lesson-laden business, fraught with consequences for punishment or reward in the future—in heaven or hell or in future lives, it is exactly the same. But to live right now, to perceive, to feel, to sense, to experience, to enjoy this moment—this, I believe, is the reason we choose to come back into a body and live in a physical world.

Sometimes, and more and more often now, when I pass a lilac in bloom, or hold someone close in my arms, or accidentally meet some stranger's eyes on a bus, a wild gladness floods my heart, and I think to myself: *this* is why I came back!

Not to learn—our spirits are perfect, already knowing everything—but to play, to experience the infinite variations on the theme of the character I am this time. Someone has said that humans are the otters of the universe. That feels right to me. I like the feeling that we have come here to this beautiful planet lightly, playfully, joyfully to experiment with the amazing possibilities of ourselves. Some of us had the extra motivation to come back of being fascinated by the on-going drama of tyranny that is being enacted here and were eager to play our part in ending it, in making that delight possible that is the natural condition of every living thing.

And of course we *do* learn. Learning is a sort of bonus, a by-product of living, not the reason for it.

"But it is the human condition to suffer," the patriarchs intone; "into every life a little rain must fall. Sweet are the uses of adversity, so be glad for your troubles, they strengthen you." No wonder the aim of practitioners of some Eastern religions is to get off the wheel of life. The fathers teach us that life, by its very nature, is full of pain and sorrow, and that this is good because only through suffering can we come to know joy, only by understanding evil can we know good. They teach us that such polarity is a law of human experience.

As usual, I ask myself, "Who said so? Who profits from the theory that polarity is an inescapable fact of life? For whom is it necessary that we accept the notion that we *need* to suffer?" The answer is obvious. Tyranny is based on suffering and on the acceptance of it by the tyrannized as "natural" and god-ordained. For sadists, polarity is a necessary and reasonable concept, and for sadists to control the world, as they do, it is necessary that this be a *universal* assumption.

But except as a weapon over the human spirit, it doesn't make any more sense than the rest of their propaganda. Suffering teaches us how to suffer—period.

There is no reason to believe that it has equal or more value in the strengthening of character than happiness has; in fact, there is reason to believe that it has less or none. I think that suffering and pain, despite patriarchy's self-serving insistence to the contrary, are not only unnecessary for health and happiness but make them impossible, that people are strong *despite* suffering, not because of it.

It seems to me likely that by reinforcing our programmed belief that it is inevitable and must simply be borne, suffering weakens us on all levels of our being. Though pain is "real" now, I am not persuaded that it *has* to be. Perhaps sorrow and pain *are made possible by,* perhaps they *result from,* patriarchy's sadistic ontology. It seems obvious to me that only joy can teach us how to be joyful, and that from joy and delight and peace we can learn all we need to know, which is how to be happy, how to rejoice, how, that is, to think about the nature of the human experience and to live on the earth in radically different terms.

People often say to me down their noses, "But Utopia would be so *boring!*" This is evidence to me of the success of a sadistic world mind in brainwashing us to believe that pain and suffering and evil are not only necessary but are also the sources of excitement and energy in life, a global ideology that equates goodness, peace, and joy with dullness and stupidity. Lucifer, in "Paradise Lost" the embodiment of evil, is supposed to dazzle us with his brilliance; in comparison with him the characters who personify "goodness" appear complete bores.

Evil in this poem, as in patriarchy, is made attractive to inure us to it. But its presentation does not make goodness more real to us. All we can know from evil is evil; it cannot teach us about goodness. Patriarchy has no concept of energized goodness, of nonpolarized and non-polarizable creativity.

I want a world in which it makes no sense at all to believe the dangerous nonsense that suffering allows us to experience joy at a deeper level, or that we learn about goodness most profoundly from studying evil. I want a world in which opposites are not even posited, in which there is no dichotomous, polarized mind. If we believe that everything is balanced by its opposite, not by its own intrinsic nature, we must always posit light and dark, male and female, rich and poor, large and small in opposi-tion—noticing that the "desirable" concept always comes first in English when we speak of polarities: light, male, rich, large; in patriarchy first position is always most desirable.

The assumption is that because these are opposites, they have naturally opposite roles to play in their spheres. In this way, the doctrine of polarity—yin/yang—is patri-archy's basic justification for tyranny.

Though theoretically polarity makes no judgments and holds that both poles are equally necessary, it is not lost on feminists that the feminine is always the negative pole, the opposite of the positive male poles. It is incredible to me, however, to what lengths some women—many of whom throw up their hands at other women who are making excuses to stay in christianity—will go to justify and rationalize and to try to make it okay to believe the same basic patriarchal structure in Eastern thought. One look at women's status and experience in the East should instantly warn us not to import indiscriminately the misogynist messages in Eastern philosophies and religions.

All we need to do to rid ourselves of rigid polar-thinking is to ask ourselves who said that dark is the *opposite* of light, therefore making possible the extension of tyranny over whole peoples? How would patriarchy change if we viewed dark and light, not as opposites at all, but as simply aspects of the same thing, variations on the same theme? The dichotomous thought necessary for oppression is based in the concept of polarity.

From women who are accepting Eastern thought without clearly recognizing its patriarchal origins, I also hear a lot of this kind of idea: "I brought this misfortune upon myself by being [a certain undesirable way] in a past life." It seems to me that this thinking lacks even a semblance of feminist analysis. It is the "blame-the-victim" mode so beloved of the elite, justifying their violence and others' poverty and misery: they deserve it, they brought it on themselves. It is a totally nonpolitical analysis, and sexual politics undergird our every act. While it is true that we collaborate as victims in oppression, collaboration is *not* causation. Our most serious collaboration is accepting patriarchy as "real" and inevitable.

Many of those who adhere to Eastern thought believe that by doing so they get completely out of christianity's way and into some extraordinary new spiritual mode. It seems to me, however, that whatever tells us that the purpose of life is for us to improve ourselves and to atone for our past sins is the same old dreary stuff the fathers have taught us under every guise. We are not good enough as we are, they say, not worthy of love yet, not enough, not enough, not enough. And because we are not enough, we must suffer until we learn to be enough and to repent of never having been enough yet. Those of us who are not enough will be ruled by those who are enough.

Though I don't agree, I don't argue with those who need to believe the disempowering "justice" dogma of some varieties of karma. No one knows the ultimate "truth" (if there is such a thing). Since none of us can know "the truth," we must each believe what we need to believe right now in order to make sense of our lives, in order to have the courage and strength to live.

But we also each need to examine and question, privately and publicly, the isms of men. Nothing men have taught as "truth" is safe for women to internalize without serious analysis. I accept none of the old stuff if I can help it, nothing from men any more. Our own internal women's voices will teach us all we need to know, and if they sound a little like Eastern thought, it is because Eastern thought still contains some of women's archaic mind. But the female mode that echoes in those philosophies has been twisted to fit male supremacy and cannot be trusted.

As my life has changed over the years and as I have come to understand more clearly the manifestations of patriarchy in my life and thought, I have changed my supporting beliefs about the nature and purpose of existence. Right now I want to be rid of my dichotomous mind, I want to be free of the idea of earth life as "school," the experiences of this present life as consequences of former lives—we all had enough of that in church. I want out of cause-and-effect thinking, out of constant projection either into the future or into the past, out of atonement, out of "justice," out of that mind. I want into a lighthearted, playful reality, finding joy in the experiences of the moment, and in fearless, disciplined thought. My belief that *being is enough* makes this possible.

CHAPTER 8

The Past Age Movement

New age ideas, though saturated with a masculinism that would be expected to deter even the least politically conscious feminists, are nevertheless seducing thousands of women of all degrees of feminist consciousness.

I believe this is because these ideas bear faint echoes from the 200,000 years of women's world that preceded patriarchy. The "new age" movement is the repository of pseudo-female Eastern thought in this country. Patriarchy has always lured women back into our prisons by dangling our own disguised precepts before us, teasing us with their familiarity. Even dimly hearing ideas that resemble the shape of women's mind causes some of us to succumb to the old subterfuge. We think we have found something wholly good and different and as if hypnotized fall back into our age-old position of listening to external male voices, either channeling them (and almost all women I know who channel entities, channel *male* entities[1]) or following male leaders. We have seen all this before. It is the by-now familiar pattern. Christianity when it began "empowered" women in just this way. But once it had captured our hearts and minds, it made no more pretense.

There is very little or no feminist consciousness among leaders of the "new age" movement. All is based upon the premise that women experience the world as men do, that there is no important or appreciable difference that merits attention. So women are invisible again, colluding again by pretending that we are really included with the men, denying our very different experience in the world, denying what male/female relationships mean at this time of the world, denying patriarchal enslavement.

The "new age" movement is the same old exploitation of women, the same old lipservice paid to the importance of our contribution in order to bring our wonderful energy, our invaluable resources of mind and spirit, under the command of men again. It is patriarchy indulging its habit of siphoning off strong women and usurping their power by taking upon itself a veneer of female values—the same old Bygone Age Movement.

---

[1] Though these voices disingenuously proclaim that they are genderless, they use male names. Even clearer evidence that they are perceived as male is that their followers refer to them as "he" and "him," never as "it." When these followers were once feminists, they—also disingenously it seems to me—vow that *they* do not think of their entity as male at all, just as christian feminists often assure me that they do not think of god or Jesus as male. There is a powerful lot of self-deception going on here.

Though more and more women are becoming aware of these tactics, our consciousness as a group is not rising in an unbroken column. We have occasional relapses, proof that our conditioned derogation of women's value is difficult for even enlightened women to overcome. A case in point was the response to the Past Age's so-called "harmonic convergence"—or "harmonica virgin," as my irreverent daughter Kari and others dubbed it.

A couple of years ago, the men who lead the past age movement, as usual pirating women's ideas and power and battening on our energy, oracularly proclaimed that the time was near when celestial bodies would be so configured that for several hours on a certain day female energy would pour forth upon the earth. Their message was so affecting that on that day all over the country people betook themselves to the most naturally powerful spot they knew of to celebrate this great event with rituals and prayers and meditation. Ironically, thousands of people who would no more listen to women than to toads celebrated women's energy when directed to do so by men.

The truth is that women's energy has been pouring forth upon this planet in the most extraordinary fullness, not for two hours, but nonstop for at least 200 years, rolling forth from all its sources in the universe— including us—like a mighty river of goodness and life. Some of us have been saying so for a long time. But because we are *women*, few men *or* women have serious- ly considered our message. It takes *men's* saying it, it takes male appropriation and management, to persuade even some feminists. We are too often still deaf to women's voices, blind to our own effect, unbelieving of our own achievements until men steal them, diminish them, and reintroduce them as their own—a major male strategy for keeping us from a knowledge of our power and stealing it from us at the same time.

When men so generously bestowed upon us a few hours of women's energy, when they purred, "Oh, celebrate the glorious feminine!" many women were deeply moved. They felt so important and powerful and proud for that short time that they handed over their power without a murmur. I heard too few women question this male perversion of the truth.

I want women to consider that nothing of value that is being said by the past age movement could even be *thought* if it weren't that women's mind has been waking for a couple of centuries, regaining its power, breaking its chains, and rising to transcendence on this planet—a phenomenon that is occurring *despite* men.

Now everywhere we hear women's values, infiltrating, saturating every movement, nearly all of which are headed by men. Women's mode of being, and our Movement—the rising of half the human race out of bondage—is what is igniting the freedom fires ablaze now around the globe. Human consciousness is expanding and finally exploding from the heat of women's liberation. All present-day insurrections take their cue and their fire from women's energy and mind.

I want women to own all this and to stop bowing at men's feet—men in this dimension or any other, to stop looking to men on any plane for leadership. I want women to recognize our own magnificent female powers of mind and spirit and to trust them without verification from the men, to start channeling our own living selves. *Nobody* outside us is wiser than we, regardless of their location in space and time. I want women, by listening to ourselves, to end this co-optation and perversion of women's material, the age-old phenomenon of men's vampiring our power, naming it their own, and using it to destroy life and joy.

Women's gratitude for the few hours of female energy men "granted" them, when they could *wallow* if they would in the illimitable quantities of it, reminded me then of some women's equally blind and humble gratitude for the UN Decade of Women that ended in 1985. We were overwhelmed that men so generously gave us permission to use ten of their 5,000-or-so years to take a little peek at ourselves—only on condition that we do it their way, of course, which effectively foiled any possibility of a global slave revolt.

Who are men that we think they can donate years to us? Do we really believe that men own time? What would happen if we believed the truth—that we could have all the decades we wanted, that we already do legitimately own them and could name them ours at any moment we took ourselves seriously enough to do it? The bestowal of the Decade upon us proves that *men* believe we could do this.

Remembering that men never do anything that will actually benefit women but only appear to, so that everything they ostensibly do for us they are really doing for themselves, we recognize the Decade as a clever stratagem to divert our rebellion into controllable channels before we realized our power and took *everything*. Men know our power far better than we do. They fear us as the masters always fear the slaves, fear our waking up in the middle of the parade and seeing that they have no clothes on, no real power. And so they must constantly develop ruses to prevent us from recognizing that their control is maintained by legerdemain. They must keep us from discovering that they are powerful and we are powerless only *because they have succeeded in making us believe it.*

Every day, however, more of us wake up to our magnificence and to the knowledge that our personal power is intensifying the fire of hope and change in which the world is being reborn. Soon men won't be able to fool any of us with such flimflam as harmonic convergences or women's decades.

CHAPTER 9

The Stars Made Me Do It

T he fact that astrology is both such an ancient science/ art and that it is based on principles of interconnectedness and interrelatedness are clues that it is one of the remnants of pre-patriarchal culture. As usual, however, crucial elements inherent in women's thinking have been replaced with nonsense.

Chief among the lost concepts is that all things in the universe influence one another and that because there is a continual flow of energy among us all, nothing has either a one-way impact or is only acted upon.

The loss of this understanding of mutuality has drastically altered everything and is responsible for the ever-increasing destruction of life on our planet. It is no wonder that it has also transmogrified astrology. As men now conceive it, heavenly bodies exert influence over the course of our lives but we do not in return effect theirs.

Whoever heard of such a thing in any other realm of the universe? Are we all connected or are we not? Are we connected with some things and not with others? If some are very large and very far away, are our spirits too small and puny to reach them? Doesn't this fly in the face of our understanding that in the atomic universe there is neither linear space nor time? Doesn't it belie women's knowledge that every existing thing is part of many ecosystems, systems inside systems inside systems that spiral on and out forever?

As untenable as it is, this notion of a one-way stream of energy is consistent with patriarchy's illogical and manipulative mind. In cahoots with the system's other concepts that persuade us to look outside ourselves for explanation and succor, this one also serves patriarchy's purpose of reinforcing our feelings of insignificance, victimization, and powerlessness: we are not the actors but the acted-upons. The stars have us by the scruffs of our necks and, though we have some minor choice in the matter, are leading us pretty much where they want us to go. We, however, have no similar say in their affairs.

But either it is true that everything is connected inseparably with everything else regardless of space or time and that therefore everything is interinfluenced by and interdependent upon everything else, or it is not true. It doesn't make sense to believe that it applies in some cases but not in others.

It is therefore reasonable to assume that our thoughts and feelings and deeds affect the courses of the stars as much, though in different ways, as theirs affect ours.

For a long time I have had the feeling that what women are accomplishing on this planet is of paramount importance to life of every kind everywhere. I have felt the glad relief of the trees as I've walked by them, have heard the river whisper "Yes, but hurry!", and watching the planets and stars appear in the evening sky, have known that their chorus of encouragement and praise for Earth's women continually rings through the universe.

I have no doubt that the course humans take has a direct and profound effect upon the direction of every atom of this and all other universes. I believe that everything that lives, including the planets and stars, is aware that their rounds are being positively and irrevocably shifted by what women are doing now on Earth, and that they are on fire with our same purpose.

So from now on, perhaps it would be more appropriate to ask not what the stars can do for us but what we can do for the stars.

CHAPTER 10

Twelve Steps Into the Fog

I n many cities across the United States, I have spoken with feminist therapists who have told me—cautiously, almost fearfully, because 12-step programs are now sacrosanct, the new religion—that these programs are not freeing the women they see in their practices. They would agree with Diana Rabenold who argues that such programs

> . . . emphasize family background and 'damaged' personal histories as the major culprits. . . at the expense of examining the political nature of the problems. Psycho-dynamic therapy lacks a cohesive analysis of power, a theory of internalized oppression . . . . An approach which over-emphasizes past and personal history often overlooks the ways in which behavior patterns are being reinforced *in*

the present by social and economic factors.[1]

To talk about social/interpersonal/political aspects of women's oppression as addiction is to keep us on a treadmill of meetings and "support" groups that don't seem to be pointing the way to liberty. All of us know women in our communities who have been in recovery groups for years, who feel as if they cannot miss a meeting, whose lives revolve around their victimization, their addiction, or their co-dependency, who align themselves with the most negative aspect of their lives by defining themselves *as* it: I am an alcoholic, I am a co-addict, I am a relationship addict, I am an incest survivor.[2]

Where is the recovery program for addiction to the 12 steps? Perhaps it is better to be dependent upon Alcoholics Anonymous than upon alcohol, but it seems to me that the better goal is to be dependent upon oneself. What I see happening in this country is that women's reliance on 12-step recovery and support groups is causing a pre-Movement fembotitude to set in.

I think we must recognize that no male institution is

---

[1] Diana Rabenold, "Love, Politics, and 'Rescue' in Lesbian Relationships," pp. 1-2.

[2] It would be a good idea to cast the word "survivor" out of our vocabularies altogether. As a relational word, as a word that throws the mind instantly back into some dread, powerless past experience(s), the word "survivor" perpetuates women's feelings of powerlessness and their perceptions of themselves as victims. Words are energy. I would like to see us use them to create our own powerful, free reality. For instance, Susan Horwitz suggests that we use the word "thrival" instead of survival.

essentially different from any other. I think we are required to hold none of them exempt from our fiercest, most self-loving scrutiny. Alcoholics Anonymous is simply another male institution, different in neither quality nor kind from the churches or schools or political parties or from any other group dedicated to maintaining men's oppressive and destructive value structure and hierarchy.

There are no new values there, nothing that is recognizable as nonparadigmatic to patriarchy. Particularly appalling for what it says about the integrity of a group that purports to care about human well-being is that there is no reverence for the body, no honor given to its health, no generalizing from the effects of alcohol to coffee and cigarettes; instead, AA exhibits as much scorn of the material world, of women's creation in it—human bodies—as any Fundamentalist church.

Recovery groups—particularly when they center around the 12 steps of AA—often have the same self-abasing, powerless, external focus, and ultimate rejection of responsibility inherent in male religion and politics. I perceive little difference between AA's "turning our will and life over to the care of God," christianity's "resting in Jesus," and the reliance of millions on legislators and presidents.

Some feminists tell me they replace "god" in the steps with "higher power," by which they often mean their "higher Self." This has no meaning for me, since apparently unlike theirs, my Self doesn't come in high, medium, and low like a hairdryer. I am whole, all of a piece, all at once. This, at least, is my desire and my direction, and therefore how I must speak of and perceive myself.

But though I cannot live as if it were true, I am aware that many of us feel as if we are still only coming together, that the wise old women inside us are still apart from us, informing and instructing us seemingly from outside our conscious minds, that there is much to be said for turning hard questions over to them and relaxing in trust, knowing that they will lead us to the answers.

In my present interaction with my wise woman, I am learning to keep hold of the reins. My role as a member of our team is to be awake and to test the assumptions at the center of my perceptions, beliefs, and behavior. I formulate the questions (sometimes needing her nudges), listen for answers, and am then very much involved, very actively part of the decision-making process. Putting the ultimate onus on anyone, anything, even on my wise old woman, would be an abnegation of responsibility that would make and keep me ill and victimized.

It is crucial for me to remember that the *conscious* Sonia is responsible for her life, no matter how strongly her Self speaks to her from what unconscious depths.

Another problem with the fact that the phrase "higher self" implies a "lower self" is that it maintains intact the hierarchical, dichotomous mind, the one-up/one-down, sadistic paradigm. In this light, the concept of a "higher" self is quintessential patriarchy. It is very important for me as a feminist to remember at all times that my wise old woman is not "higher." She is my peer.

The addiction movement's ideas seem to me to come

out of a mind very like that of Fundamentalist religionists. I see no important difference between the addiction addicts who say, "You are all *sick!*" and the preachers who thunder, "You are all *sinners!*" It is the same model. The political model, the medical/therapeutic model, the religious model—all of them the patriarchal model.

In this model, norms are based on "sick" people, on victims. When sickness is the norm and we are all sick, the perception is that sickness is inevitable, that we can never be entirely well, and certainly can never save ourselves but need ministers and doctors and therapists and countless programs and support groups to rescue us and keep us at coping level.

And that we need them not just for awhile but for years or even for most of our lives, because, we are told, once born we are always sinners, once alcoholics we are always alcoholics, once victimized in whatever way, we are victims for life. In this way we can always put the blame for our misery on something external, refuse responsibility, and choose to be weak, unable to stand on our own, in constant need of support, never free.

It seems to me that in such groups women's lives center around a healing that is perpetual, that can never be completed: recovery programs in which no one ever recovers, in which recovery is not even the goal, not even considered a possibility, programs, in fact, in which to be a "good" and accepted member one must always assert one's illness, one's pain, one's inability to recover.

In patriarchal models, health and joy are not posited as options; we can only hope to be less unwell, in less pain, to cope, to have ordinary lives.

But, obviously, concentrating on sickness can never make us well, any more than concentrating on sinfulness can make us feel worthy. Defining ourselves *as* our oppression both *in*ternalizes and *e*ternalizes our oppression, viewing ourselves as sick keeps us sick. To keep us from finding the tools of liberation, patriarchy always begins from sickness to describe "health," from addiction to describe liberation.

Feminism, the most profound deprogramming, the most thorough revolution of ideas, thoughts, and feelings the world has ever experienced, does not allow us to underestimate the scale and depth of patriarchal conditioning in our lives; it will not let us go to sleep again. It will not allow me to speak of its enormity, as it manifests itself in our every interaction with ourselves, others, and the world, in the same breath as I speak of addictions to chocolate or even to alcohol or cocaine.

When in the past I have ventured hesitantly to say to true 12-step believers that "the program" seemed overpoweringly in the old paradigm, they have pooh-poohed me into silence. "I just ignore all that stuff," they shrug. But they can only have said that out of an ignorance of the dynamics of terror-induced brainwashing, out of ignorance of its subtlety, its pervasiveness, its invasiveness.

Or out of denial. Like women in the churches, like women in the political parties, like women in the universities, women who belong to any organizations set up on male models to serve men, they woefully underestimate their vulnerability to the barrage of propagandistic disease and psychic maiming that rips into them from the very sectors to which they have turned for health and wholeness and "support."

In order to do this, they must accept the patriarchal chicanery that meaning can be separated from form. The fact is that meaning and form are inextricably fused. Meaning dictates form; in return the form, when it is not the entire meaning, is always a significant part of it. Form and meaning are causally intertwined in such a way that to understand one the other must always be taken into account. Since the form of AA, churches, and universities is patriarchal, any overt nonpatriarchal meanings that may be conveyed there will be canceled out by the meanings inherent in the format (for instance, hierarchical and competitive), the purpose, the setting, the values expressed by the format, purpose, and setting, and so on.

Members of AA talk a good deal about "denial," but I have noticed that women who are ardent worshipers at the foot of the 12 steps—"It saved my *life!*"—fiercely deny the profoundly masculinist world view inherent in those steps.

What is most noticeable about the steps at first reading, for example, is their thoroughgoing negativity: in the first step the words "powerlessness" and "unmanageable" appear; in subsequent steps, adherents guiltily confess to "wrongs," "defects," "shortcomings," admit having "harmed" and "injured," and concentrate upon making "amends" and on admitting when they are "wrong." The steps fairly groan under their load of self-abasement.

Women want and need a new world, a life ennobled by self-love. We do not need further humbling. For 5,000 long years, men have carefully trained our eyes upon our shortcomings and our faults, our evil proclivities and our weaknesses. They have taught us how to scrutinize ourselves for wicked intent and behavior so well that we came long ago to the point of searching out faults we didn't even have, inventing shortcomings to please the men, to feel righteous and god-fearing. We learned our lesson of self-hatred all too well.

We do not need to look any longer at what is wrong with us, because as long as we do we will never rise out of the slough. We need to see what we are doing *right*, what we are doing that is strong and good and loving and free. *That's* the "fearless inventory" [3] women need to make of our lives.

And then, of course, the woman-hating male god lurks in nearly every line of the 12 steps, ready to pounce upon the unwary, vulnerable psyche, the maleficent presence that women in AA-like programs (and churches) deny changes their feelings about themselves at all. I often wonder what makes them more immune to brainwashing than the rest of us. Although the steps purport to give one the option of thinking of god as one wishes, the text is riddled with unambiguous male god concepts and lan-

---

[3] One of the 12 Steps is that people will make fearless inventories of their lives.

guage, saturated with a rigid patriarchal world view.

It is also very other-directed. Since men have not been socialized to think of others, to be as concerned about the welfare of others to the extent women have, this may be fine for them. But women, who have been deeply conditioned to put everyone else's needs and wants before their own, to take responsibility for everyone and everything except their own freedom and happiness, women, who apologize when men step on their feet or run into them, who apologize to posts they run into—women need to *stop* feeling apologetic about living and learn to think of and put their own welfare first. They need no more brainwashing to consider others' lives, no more mandates to apologize.

Negativity, remorse, repentance, giving up of ultimate responsibility—i.e., immersion in patriarchal power politics—can never lead to independence and personal power, can never free from conditioned assumptions.

"But," women protest, "the 12 steps help *me*! And my reality is valid for me." I was once a Mormon, and for a large part of my life I perceived the church as "helping" me. I had what I thought of as "spiritual experiences" in relation to it. I had what I regarded as answers to prayer. But when I no longer believed in god, when I no longer thought the church was holy and full of power, I sat on its benches and felt shocked at its barrenness, its echoing emptiness.

I knew then that what I had once regarded as the doctrine's rich, sacred, and transcendent stuff was in reality my *own* rich, sacred, and transcendent stuff: I had answered my own prayers, I had filled the church with my own glory. But I had projected all this onto the church because I could not conceive of myself as so powerful. I could not accept my own divinity. I had been taught to externalize my power and to call it god and his priesthood, to give it up to that figment and his priests so that I could never claim it for myself. By doing so, women threaten to bring down the whole house of cards around the men's heads.

Neither AA nor any other patriarchal organization will ever be the first with the good news about how to make deep and lasting change in our lives and in the world. In my opinion, women who get well through AA get well because they so desire health that out of themselves they pull the threads of self-love that form their web of safety. I believe that motivated women have learned to use any impetus, any excuse, to grab any plank in the heaving seas, to get well. Unfortunately, AA has been almost the only plank floating by.

Women have been angry when I have said this about AA, insisting that though they can see all its defects, it has after all helped many women, and they are glad that it is there. I tell them that during my long life as a Mormon I heard countless people bear testimony that the church had saved their lives, but I do not now conclude, for example, that because Mormonism keeps millions of people from drinking, everyone with a drinking problem should join it.

These women then often respond that they know AA is not good in many ways, but it is already there and they are too frazzled from trying to make a living to take on organizing some group based on more feminist principles. Now *that* seems to me a far more legitimate reason for a woman's attending AA than any other I have heard.

Fortunately, at least one group other than the depressingly moralistic christian AA exists for women with drinking problems, a group based on the knowledge that men's comfortable reality is alien territory for women.

Though I could wish that it contained a more thoroughgoing woman-centered political analysis, Women for Sobriety, a national organization exclusively for women *is* based on the understanding that women have been programmed differently from men in patriarchy and that feelings of self-worth, not self-mortification, are basic to our ability to free ourselves from alcohol.

Women for Sobriety's 13 steps[4] are as different from men's 12 as night from day. They are present-time oriented (women are not asked to rehearse their drinking histories), positive, self-affirming and self-directed, guilt-free, and have some metaphysical sophistication:

1) I have a drinking problem that once had me.
2) Negative emotions destroy only myself.
3) Happiness is a habit I can develop.
4) Problems bother me only to the degree that I permit them in.

---

[4] The 13 statements were originally published in Dr. Jean Kirkpatrick's book, *Turnabout: Help for a New Life*. Doubleday and Co: New York, 1978.

5) I am what I think.
6) Life can be ordinary or it can be great.
7) Love can change the course of my world.
8) The fundamental object of life is emotional and spiritual growth.
9) The past is gone forever.
10) All love given returns two-fold.
11) Enthusiasm is my daily exercise.
12) I am a competent woman and have much to give others.
13) I am responsible for myself and my sisters.

This program keeps what is good about AA and dumps the rest. Using women's life experience as the norm, it is designed by a woman specifically to give women what they need to recover—insisting on women-only meetings, for instance. Jean Kirkpatrick, founder of Women for Sobriety, understands that women's problems "are tied to the male-female relationship" [5] and that these problems cannot be thoroughly explored in a mixed group; that in mixed groups men do most of the talking, giving women little chance to speak about what is bothering them; and that men consider women's frustrations—crying children, no adult company—petty and boring and not deserving of a place in the general discussion. In short, patriarchy prevails in AA as it does in most mixed support groups.[6]

[5] Jean Kirkpatrick, *Women for Sobriety: A New Self-Help Program*, 1978.

[6] Jean Kirkpatrick, *Women for Sobriety: A New Self-Help Program*, 1978.

But according to Kirkpatrick, the most disabling patriarchal characteristic of 12-step programs for women is that they attack their already diminished self-esteem. Recognizing that a woman's self-image is the most accurate predictor of her ability to change, Kirkpatrick tried consciously to build positive steps toward self-respect and independence into Women for Sobriety.

"The program is an affirmation of the value and worth of each woman," she writes.

> It leads each woman to assert her belief in herself, to see herself in a positive and self-confident light, as forceful and compassionate, assertive and warm, capable and caring, resourceful and responsible.[7]

Kirkpatrick, an active alcoholic herself for 28 years, tried nearly every available therapy, dropping twice out of AA. By the time she kicked the habit, she was convinced that none of the programs addressed the problems of America's five million women alcoholics.[8] In her opinion,

> All women in our culture feel a modicum of guilt for not being "perfect," for not fitting into the unrealistic mold that American society has cast for them. For alcoholic women, this guilt is almost unbearable at times. When the feelings about this guilt are shared with other women who

---

[7] Jean Kirkpatrick, *Turnabout: Help for a New Life*, p. 64.

[8] "Finding AA Too Male-Oriented, Jean Kirkpatrick Heads a Movement to Aid Women Alcoholics," *People Magazine*, June 29, 1987.

also experience it, it can be alleviated, become a thing of the past. Women alcoholics have this strong feeling of having failed as a wife, as a mother, as a sister or daughter, as a woman. Their alcoholism and recovery are all involved with the removal of this guilt.[9]

She believes that the reasons men and women drink are also entirely different. "Men drink for a sense of power," she says, "while women drink out of frustration, helplessness and dependency." [10]

In Women for Sobriety groups, women introduce themselves by affirming their dignity and self-respect: "My name is Jean and I'm a competent woman." Instead of repeating the lord's prayer, they conclude their meetings by joining hands and affirming: "We are capable and confident, caring and compassionate, always willing to help another, bonded together in overcoming our disease of alcoholism."

Another difference is that this group, in a more holistic, womanly sort of way, is interested in improving and maintaining each woman's health in every way, not merely in keeping her alcoholism at coping level. Part of the program emphasis, for instance, is "the use of meditation, taking vitamins, avoiding candy, drinking little or no coffee, and cutting down on smoking"—i.e., loving oneself, including her body, and taking her body and

[9] Jean Kirkpatrick, *Turnabout: Help For a New Life*, p. 83.

[10] "Finding AA Too Male-Oriented, Jean Kirkpatrick Heads a Movement to Aid Women Alcoholics."

health seriously.[11]

But predictably enough, Women for Sobriety gets little recognition and less prestige, primarily because it does not include men, and almost none of us is able to take women-only groups as seriously as we do those that include men. Neither is it based in men's value system. It is unacceptable and even fear provoking because it comes out of women's mind, is based on women's experience, and is directed toward women.

Because it does not have the masters' imprimatur, because it is positive and affirming and therefore does not sound familiarly and comfortably like patriarchy, many doubt its efficacy. AA goes beyond this and actively persecutes individual members as well as the organization itself.[12] It is very hard for women to believe that women understand us better, know better what we need, and can provide it better than men— evidence of our internalized oppression, our self-hatred, our slave mind.

Why has men's 12-step program—negative, other-directed, conventionally blaming the victim, mortifying and abasing, god-oriented—been perceived by some women as life-changing? Perhaps it feels comfortable and right to women precisely because it *is* the same old externalization of power, the same old powerlessness, the same old negativity, the same old moralistic, abject, lack of self-love (any feminist who sits through the lord's

---

[11] To contact Women for Sobriety, write P. O. Box 618, Quakertown, PA, 18951, or call (215) 536-8026.

[12] Conversation with Jean Kirkpatrick, August 1988.

prayer several times a week—even once a *year*—does not honor herself much in my opinion), and when we are in pain we find solace in the known, in the echoes from our childhood.

But more likely women find strength in any 12-step program simply because it *is* a program. When we feel as if our lives are out of our control, when we are in emotional chaos, finding such a solid, rigid structure must feel like coming upon a life raft in a shipwreck. Perhaps it didn't need to be the 12 steps of AA for those people to feel so welcome and safe; perhaps the relief would have been the same if *any* process had appeared, any dependable program in which there was group support and acceptance. As I say, thousands of people join the Mormon church yearly for this exact reason.

Though the Women's Movement began with consciousness-raising groups, since then it hasn't answered the conditioned need for external structure, programs, dogma, and ritual. Feminism has routinely required each of us to bring this forth for ourselves out of ourselves, but never insisted that we not have company as we do it.

Doing our own individual internal work, whether alone or with a group, is extremely difficult. In patriarchy, we are accustomed to having someone else set up for us what we need to do—parents, churches, schools, preachers, nuns, teachers, TV ads, how-to-do-it manuals—it seems as if in every direction we turn we are being told what to do and how to do it, given a regimen to follow: to get good grades, to win god's approval, to lose weight, to keep fit, to have satisfying sex. We hardly need to listen to our own internal voices at all anymore; certainly society neither encourages nor gives us any practice.

So it isn't surprising that women are attracted to one more program telling us how to get our lives in order, trusting in yet another externally imposed blueprint for success, rather than accepting that it is finally necessary for each of us to find our own internal map, to listen to our own voice, and to establish our own unique and individual regimen. Following someone else's plan has never yet worked for us, and I think never will, though we might get some ideas from it.

But we *do* need one another, we do need to be in the company of other women on similar journeys. Perhaps this is why the women's spirituality movement is having such success. It may be a group process that is providing a transition from the outer-directed, externally structured patriarchal world to the less structured, more ambiguous, freer, more open and ever-changing inner world. I believe that feminism postulates anarchy of the spirit—self-rule, self-government, an anarchy that will ultimately result in political, social, economic, and religious anarchy.

CHAPTER 11

We Are *Not* Sick!

Nineteen eighty-eight was the heyday of the addiction experts. They were everywhere, solemnly assuring us that the villain in our lives was co-dependency and that to banish it we all needed a support group—or two or three—of the 12-step variety.

But some of us were not convinced. We had observed our women friends who were devotees of these groups and we hadn't liked much of what we had seen. What disturbed me most was that the thinking of many of these women seemed to become more and more conventional, less and less adventurous, with every meeting.

As I thought about it, I concluded that 12-step programs fail to encourage emotional daring and independence in women primarily because both the addiction model and the terminology of its attendant theory are powerless before the depth and scope of our internalized bondage. They are unable either to explain or to soothe the heartache we suffer all our lives from harboring the self-hatred that is patriarchy in our souls.

Radical feminism posits that patriarchy is the poisoned well from which all maladies and miseries flow. It is neither a disease nor a substance. To reduce it to an addiction propagated by white males, or to the "dysfunctional family," not only trivializes it, but also obscures its true character: *sadism* is patriarchy's basic social pathology.

It should come as no surprise that the addiction model does not address sadism. No model coming out of patriarchy as this one does is going to take on hierarchy in any historically or politically accurate way. I personally refuse to use addiction terminology because, like all patriarchal dialects, it is designed to cloak the political realities of oppression in women's lives.

Patriarchy is hierarchy and hierarchy is oppression—a basic feminist contribution to modern thought. Patriarchy is also a *particular* hierarchy/oppression, a world view and global ontology that translates into an omniracial, omninational, omniclass system of female slavery. It is a terrorist regime in which females are kept internally subjugated from birth by continuous threats of external assault and murder.

Mere threats, however, could never have achieved the degree of terror-based compliance we observe and experience in ourselves and in other women. Patriarchy is a deadly serious, brilliantly organized and endlessly funded all-out war against women; total war against our bodies, our minds, our spirits, our emotions, against the very essence of our femaleness. For millennia we have been prisoners of war almost everywhere on this planet, political prisoners, hostages. And as such, from birth we are unceasingly tortured: raped, incested, sexually enslaved, humiliated, impoverished, battered, verbally assaulted, sexually harassed, ignored or viewed as sources of amusement, regarded as nonhuman—objects—and as nonindividuals—clones, scapegoated for all men's failures, and murdered.

We are not only tortured in the ways *men* define torture but also in many ways that only *we* recognize. We are, for instance, tortured by having to use our masters' woman-loathing language, by trying to express our boundless slave sorrow in an alien and hostile tongue in which there are no words large enough, strong enough, brave enough to mourn or to celebrate our courageous, our splendid out-caste women's lives.

Like all prisoners, under torture we have bonded with our torturers against ourselves and one another, internalizing men's hatred of us and to some degree or another applying their model of subjugation to all our interactions.

Therefore, to shrink patriarchy to a "dysfunction," to list aspects of this unspeakably monstrous daily experience of millions of tortured women over many millennia, as various "addictions"—addictions to relationships, to food, to sex, to love, to power, to men, to security, to abuse, as well as to drugs—is to give evidence of the nonseriousness, the total lack of respect with which our lives are regarded. It is as dishonorable as calling the plight of South African Blacks, or Jews in Nazi Germany, "addiction." In so belittling our experience, in ignoring both its political context and content, calling gynecide "addiction" effectively erases it.

Dominance and subordination—sadism—is not an addiction. It is an artifact and tool of global patriarchal culture as well as its modus operandi; it is a model that saturates all our thought and behavior, planet Earth's prevailing paradigm.

To maintain that nearly every problem is either an addiction or the result of one, to assert that addiction is the major category of which all else are specific examples—this is not only immoral but ludicrously inaccurate. *Oppression* is the category, addiction one specific example or manifestation of *it*. Addiction is possible *because of* oppression, not the other way around.

Oppression is maintained, not through addiction, but through conditioning, through brainwashing. Hierarchy/tyranny, totally dependent upon brainwashing, is promulgated and perpetuated by it in every aspect of our culture and society. Conditioning defines human nature, our relationships to one another, ourselves, the universe, the divine. It dictates every assumption on which we base our lives. It is the way a world view is maintained, the way "reality" is structured and accepted. Both oppression and its minion, brainwashing, are virtually invisible and thoroughly invasive, assaulting every cell of our bodies and minds.

Our conditioning determines what we see and what is not evident to us, what we deem possible, what we consider important, what we pay attention to, what we believe—i.e., how we live every moment of our lives, *all* of us. There is already and has always been another reality in our midst, one of beauty and peace, happiness and power, kindness, abundance, and creative joy. Our brainwashing is what keeps us from seeing and living in that world right now though it is all around us, *right before our eyes,* present and available, just as "real" as our hands in front of our faces, as real as the beating of our hearts this moment, our blood pounding through our arteries.

Brainwashing, not addiction, is what is keeping every member of the human race in thrall, in total and grimmest captivity.

Naming this phenomenon "addiction" would be laughable if it were not so irresponsible and dangerous, preventing as it does our picking up the tools with which to free ourselves. To talk about social/interpersonal/political aspects of women's bondage as addiction is to deprive us of the equipment necessary to do our relationships differently, to dismantle patriarchy within them and within our lives.

The incalculable gift of feminism to women and to the world is the clarity with which it reveals misogyny as systemic, not as an isolated problem of individual women brought about by their being "addictive personalities" or "co-addicts" or by lack of courage or by general worthlessness or ineptitude or because of hereditary weakness or by membership in a "dysfunctional family." [1]

Feminism, by depersonalizing women's bondage and generalizing our experience, refuses to blame the victim. Feminism tells us that it is not a matter of blame but rather of looking bravely at the truth of our lives. And the truth is that there are perpetrators, there are those who profit, and profit hugely—materially and psychically—from our subjugation.

Feminism provides us with the knowledge that women in every sizable society in the world and most of the others are kept enslaved by massive violence, by brutality so implacable, on such a scale and to such a depth that it is, for most of us, not wholly imaginable, barely thinkable. Teaching us that as women we were deliberately *made* slaves, helping us understand how we are deliberately *kept* slaves, and promising that we can end our slavery, feminism hands us three essential tools: truth, self-esteem, and hope.

The genius of radical feminist theory is its understanding of the "seasoning" of women to be slaves, of the training of men to be masters, of the consequent total corruption of perception, thought, and feeling, and therefore of human liberty on every level of life.

Any hypothesis, any explanation of our difficulty not based on or considering or recognizing the centrality of radical feminist theory, ignoring that all thought forms and institutions, all private and public behavior are

---

[1] As if *any* institution of patriarchy can be said to "function" to promote human well-being on any level!

gender-control based and set up to maintain the slave economy of the planet, cannot finally point the way to liberty for anyone. Any such theory is, in fact, harmful in its denial, in its erasure, of the political, social, and economic facts, of the structure of women's public and private lives in every race, every class, every nation of the world.

This structure, this system, may have been brought to its acme by white men, but men of all races and classes have perpetuated it with singular virulence for thousands of years. Chinese men seasoned Chinese women to maim each other horribly for one thousand years, hundreds of years before white men became ascendant in the world. Black men brainwashed Black women to punish themselves for being sexually creative, for having the power to give birth, by cutting their genitalia off and out. These women were not and are not addicted to such self-mutilation. Evidence that it is a conditioned response is that their behavior was at the time, and still is in many cultures, perceived by most people as "natural," inescapable, inevitable—reality—and the necessity for it *felt* as a matter of life and death.

The element of choice and the absence of perpetrators is perhaps what most distinguishes addiction from conditioning. Choice enters into physical/medical addiction in a way that it does not enter at all in the brainwashing necessary for oppression. Nobody *makes* us an addict. Despite massive propaganda to become dependent upon some substance, despite foreign troops' bringing drug wars to our inner cities, many people are *not* addicted: do not smoke cigarettes or pot, do not drink alcohol or coffee or tea or colas, do not take tranquilizers or other addicting "legal" drugs or meddle with street or designer drugs. Though circumstances can be extremely conducive, outside of actual torture chambers no one can finally be *forced* to become an addict.

In the absolutely pervasive global brainwashing to hate women and all things womanly, however, there *are* perpetrators and *everyone* is profoundly affected. For all of us, it begins at birth and there is no escape, no choice. The men who control the world brainwash everyone to a greater or lesser degree—as they themselves have been brainwashed; they brainwash everyone thoroughly enough for patriarchy to have gone lurching along for 5,000 wretched years.

There is also an enormous difference between oppression and addiction in the process and difficulty of recovery. Brainwashing is invisible on every level, addiction is not. Despite the denial that *we* are addicted, we see that others are, we can *see* addiction; our own condition may be invisible to us, but addiction itself is not invisible. And when we stop denying and choose to rid ourselves of it, we can and do. We either stop smoking, stop drinking, stop using cocaine or taking Valium, or we don't. It is clear whether we have or not, if not to ourselves, at least to those around us.

No one underestimates the difficulty of breaking a physical addiction, but it is nevertheless done every day by thousands of people. Though hard to break, these habits have a decided, luxurious simplicity about them not true of the process men obfuscate by naming "socialization" and that feminists clarify by calling brainwashing, conditioning, seasoning.

Because of the invisibility that renders it effectively nonexistent, keeping it a nonissue for most people, and because of its total camouflaging pervasiveness, deprogramming is far more difficult than becoming non-addicted—is in fact part of recovering from any addiction; it is perhaps the most difficult of all human acts. To discover the assumption, to posit other possibilities, to perceive, to *feel*, and to believe another reality while being blasted with this one—in short, to recreate oneself and the universe from scratch—this is what is required to "recover" from the brainwashing of oppression. Viewing addiction as The Problem, rather than as one symptom of the problem that is patriarchal oppression, ensures the invisibility of male supremacy and *actively* oppresses women.

This is to say that calling all patriarchy's manifestations the result of addiction is to have no feminist political analysis and therefore to be part of the cover-up, to collude in and perpetuate the brainwashing necessary for patriarchy's survival.

At the base of the social addiction model that has been extrapolated from the medical model lies the assumption that males and females of the same class and race have essentially the same experience in a society. This assumption, by making women as a caste invisible again, succeeds in disorienting and confusing us. Female alcoholics, for instance, do *not* have the same experience with alcohol as male alcoholics of their same social level and race; every moment of it is colored, predetermined, if you will, by the fact of their inferior status and the consequent skewing of their internal worlds.

Male children of alcoholics do *not* have the same experience in any family as female children. Though they may have horrible ordeals, their maleness causes these to be *different* ordeals—both in fact and in perception.

In AA, as in most mixed recovery groups, the reality of the uniqueness of female experience is obscured if not altogether obliterated. The obliviousness to gender-based privilege in these groups is keeping male reality the norm to which women must conform once again, is losing women to our identity again, hooking us back into patriarchal forms and values and diverting us from our own movement.

Among the most unsettling features of using the physical addiction model to describe nearly every un-pleasant phenomenon is that addiction has become, at this time in the history of the disenfranchised and emarginated people of color of the inner cities, for instance, a matter, not of overeating or loving too much, but of genocide. To call such primarily white, middle-class problems as these "addictions" seems not only preemptive but callous. In the face of the grief and confusion, the unspeakable anguish of families of any color who have one or more members with brains permanently scrambled by PCP or horribly dead from physiological addiction, of desperate human beings whose neighborhoods are occupied by foreign armies of drug dealers waging war against their children, of families who are taking a long bath in hell and can't see any way out—in the face of this nightmare, to lump all societal problems together as "addictions" is to make a mockery of those who are suffering lives shattered by addiction and carelessly to erase their experience.[2]

Another major objection to using the medical addiction model to describe nearly everything wrong is that it gives women the most disabling message possible: you are sick. In patriarchy, to be female is automatically to be "not well." Every day in thousands of ways men's system conveys to every living woman that femaleness is a disease, a disgusting, hideous deformity, and encourages us in every way possible to get "well"—to turn into silicon Stepford Wives or junior men.

Assuring us that our dissatisfaction with society is sickness, that our refusal to conform and be totally obliterated is sickness, patriarchy attempts to "cure" us of our outrageous and dangerous womanliness with guilt and blame and therapists and institutions and shock treatments.

For this reason, unless I am speaking of illness that is physically manifested, I do not choose to use the term "healing," as in "healing ourselves." Though women have been ferociously brainwashed and abused by a sick culture, the distinction is that *it* is sick, not *us*. We are oppressed, we are nonfree, but we are not sick. I under-

---

[2] Conversation with Mary Ann Beall, August 1988.

stand why women use the word "healing," and I know that for many of them it seems to have very positive connotations. But I also know that healing presupposes illness and that patriarchy teaches us to view ourselves as sick and weak and vulnerable so that we will then behave weakly and vulnerably.

So hearing everywhere again nowadays that we are all sick in one way or another, all addicted to something, sets my alarm bells clanging. I know that the sickness model does not come from women's culture. Because obsession with—fear and consequent causation of—sickness and death on every hand is men's contribution to the world, perceiving the world in terms of individual responsibility instead of co-dependency changes reality. To affirm health and joy and freedom as our norms is to make health and joy and freedom possible.

No matter what new person's throat they come out of, I recognize those old voices that tell me I am addicted and sick, and I don't trust them. They are the voices that lied to me in the past. But I hear a voice in my soul that never lies to me, a voice I know I can trust. That voice says very clearly and unequivocally that *I am not addicted to anything*—relationships, food, drugs, endorphins, or sex. I am not and never have been co-dependent. Though it tells me that I have been, like every living woman, deeply programmed, it also congratulates me for daily freeing myself of old assumptions and patterns that keep me tied to patriarchy.

My inner voice also assures me that I am not sick, but instead am robust and strong, becoming stronger by the hour.

Women are not sick; *we are brainwashed.* The difference is critical. It is the difference between success of the She/Volution and failure, the difference between life and death.

CHAPTER 12

The Scarlet O'Hara School of Social Change

Women often ask me to tell them what they should do to change the world. When I suggest that they should live today according to the values they wish governed the world, they often turn away to hide their disappointment.

I suppose I could tell them that we definitely cannot change the world by doing more of the same things we have been doing. I could predict that we are each going to have to continue to live our own individual, private lives in a radically different way. I could explain that the least of this is that we are each going to have to begin following whatever path it is that we already know is a more advanced way for us, paths that will refine and sculpt us into the women we not only desire to be but must be to fulfill our destinies.

But too often women who assure me fervently that their greatest passion is to change the world and who are well along in their internal revolutions are still not living with full integrity in their own personal worlds. They do not want to think today about making the changes they know they must make; like Scarlet they plan to think about it tomorrow.

But tomorrow will never come. So it is critical to live *now* as we know we should: scrutinizing our personal relationships for damaging emotional clutter and cleaning it up; resisting acquisitiveness by not piling up the "mountains of things" Tracy Chapman sings to warn us about; performing such simple and transformative acts as recycling everything recyclable, conserving water and other resources, walking and bicycling whenever possible, and generally simplifying our lives; discovering and claiming our full spiritual selves; respecting and listening to other women; honoring our bodies by eating correctly (an immensely political act—if not being totally vege-tarian, for instance, then at the very least refusing to eat meat from commercially-raised animals), getting enough rest and exercise, laughing often, and—particular-ly—breaking addictions to such destructive substances as nicotine, caffeine, alcohol, sugar, marijuana, anti-depressants, and tranquilizers.

Women all over the country are facing up to addic-tions and trying to break them. Certainly no one would argue that addictions help us free ourselves. Yet I hear feminists whom I perceive as earnestly engaged in the search for freedom say, for instance, "I can't get started in the morning without my coffee," or "food always tastes better with wine," or "marijuana is a nonaddictive, spirituality-enhancing herb," [1] or "I can't get to sleep without Valium." Where we have to start breaking free is from our coziest chains—our morning coffee, our evening drink or smoke, our liqueur with dessert. These are patriarchy's implements to stupefy and finally to incapacitate us, not to mention its diabolical scheme to use our money to destroy our own and others' lives.

If we want a world in which no one's life or health is destroyed by habituating substances, we must make that world possible now in our own private lives and as a group and Movement. Knowing that at least 50 percent of Lesbians have problems with alcohol, and that many women are at this moment freeing themselves of addictions by great and difficult dedication to loving themselves, we show respect for them and celebrate their move along the path to freedom by serving only healthful food and drinks at our functions.

It is reasonable to ask that our events demonstrate our rethinking of values and conventions, that they model a new way of relating to ourselves and others, that they prove that we take women's lives and health seriously.

This suggestion is often countered with concern about curtailing freedoms and about not accepting "difference." But these arguments no longer tempt me to connive in or

---

[1] Many women have told me of their struggle to break free of marijuana. Those who believe it is not addictive need to follow me from speech to speech and hear some personal testimonies about its destructiveness in women's lives.

to condone other women's self-destruction. I think we need to be clear about this. We need to be clear that it is all right to make judgments and decisions based on our beliefs. Sometimes *not* judging is cruel and irresponsible.

If we are alarmed that this allows no choice, we need to remember that when we plan events we can at best provide for a finite number of choices. Since we will have to leave out most things anyway—no one worries about not providing frijoles, for example, or cucumber sandwiches—let us leave out what we know does not promote women's health. By paying respect to, by honoring these bodies of ours, we take a giant step out of patriarchy.

Each one of us knows at least a dozen more obvious ways we could live according to our biophilic value system, more aware of all other life forms, more connected to them and to ourselves. The only way I have found of becoming more conscious is by acting on the consciousness I already have. If there is a better way of refining the perceptions, the senses, and the judgment, I haven't heard of it.

And unless we begin to practice *today* what we already know is most respectful and loving of ourselves and others, we cannot expect our witch/goddess Selves to reveal further ways to us *tomorrow*.

Treading water is good exercise but it's boring and it doesn't get anyone anywhere in particular.

CHAPTER 13

Motherhood: The Last Taboo

S ometimes when I want to break quickly through the
social facade of a woman who is a mother, I quietly
drop into the conversation something like "Motherhood is
terrible, isn't it?" Although there are always a few who
exclaim in shocked tones, "Oh no, I think it's *wonderful*,"
I am surprised how often women will dispense with all
pretense and admit, sometimes with tears, that yes, it *is*
terrible. Or look at me in surprise and, seeing that I am
serious, admit with relief, "It's a nightmare!"

Some mothers tell me that, though their experience
has been agonizing, they believe they have learned lessons
from it that they could have learned in no other way. I
agree that I have learned from it but any positive lessons
I learned I could have learned in other ways and the many
negative habits patriarchal motherhood reinforced—such
as self-sacrifice—I could have done without altogether.

As is true of all other experiences in life, motherhood is not the means to some other end, a way, for instance, to learn to be a more patient, more loving person. It must satisfy our needs for thoughtful engagement, creativity, pleasure, and freedom every moment or it is neither good for us nor for children. That it meets so few of these needs so little of the time is evidence that it is not as it should be and that we collaborate by being involved in it *as it is*.

Since motherhood was the original battleground of patriarchy, it is small wonder that it is now fraught with tumultuous emotions, contradictions, misperceptions, and illusions. Or that there is terrific denial among women about the reality of the motherhood experience. It has been made our sine qua non; more than that, our raison d'etre, and, accepting this, we have an enormous stake in believing all men's lies about it.

But I have thought about it for 26 years, and though I know every woman's experience is unique, I have heard enough mothers' confessions to know that I am not alone in my conclusions.

I hardly need point out that this is not because our children are not lovable or that we do not love them thoroughly. Nor do I need to point out that finding motherhood unbearable in patriarchy is to admit that one is not a worthy woman, not a decent, kind, valuable human being, making us afraid to be honest with one another about motherhood, afraid to feel, let alone to admit, how desperately oppressive it is, what a torture rack men have made of it to punish us for our greater creative powers.

Even in the Women's Movement to admit this is taboo. Even among ourselves we fear that not kneeling at the motherhood shrine will make us look weak and incompetent and unfeeling. We are afraid that if we speak the truth of our lives as mothers, we will find ourselves standing alone, the unnatural, scorned exception; that if we were to tell what agony motherhood has been for us, women of all political persuasions might fall upon us in rage, so invested are women in keeping the fathers' last guilty secret: that making motherhood horrific while brainwashing us to believe instead that it is beatific, they have effectively secured our minds and hearts, our cooperation.

When Ann Landers asked parents to write in and tell her whether they would have children if they could do it all over again, she received 10,000 replies. Because they could be anonymous, 70 percent said unequivocally, "Not on your life!" I suspect the merest fraction of that number would have admitted this if they had thought their friends or relatives would find out.

What is the matter with motherhood? I'm *certain* that nothing is intrinsically woman-destroying about it, that it could be marvelous for both mothers and children. But something is desperately wrong with motherhood as a patriarchal institution. Patriarchy, after all, arose in history as men's response to the power of women as mothers. A substantial part of its purpose, therefore, was to subvert motherhood, to plunge it from the apex of status and esteem to the nadir, to make mothers, instead of the *most*, the *least* important, *least* credible people in society, therefore *least* able to influence anyone, including and most especially the children whom fathers had so recently come to own.

And then, turning the screw, they programmed women to believe that motherhood defined us completely, that if we didn't have children, we were nobody. We have been caught in a classic double bind ever since—we are nobody if we *are* mothers, nobody if we *aren't*.

The agony of motherhood in patriarchy is that we are prevented from mothering our children. Looking back after four children and 26 years of motherhood, it seems to me that the moment I had my babies, society tied my hands and feet, stuffed a sock in my mouth, and forced me to sit helplessly by while it systematically tortured and brainwashed and poisoned my children. Men have reduced mothering to feeding, clothing, and comforting— and suffering because this is not enough. It is neither what women are capable of nor need mothering to be.

It seems to me that mothering is the business of making the world amenable to children, seeing to it, for example, that every child born is immensely valued for being exactly who they are, making a world in which they therefore automatically love and cherish themselves, a safe, wholesome, healthful world, a world in which they can cooperate, not compete, can have time to be children, are encouraged to listen to their own voices so they will learn to have integrity and to rule themselves with wisdom and mercy, a world in which they can be themselves fully.

I want a world in which women can *mother*, not just bear children and keep them alive the best we can in a world that hates them and wants to kill them because they are ours. *That* is patriarchy's definition of motherhood, not mine.

Patriarchy continues to define for women what we want, continues to control the discussion of mothering. Which of us, for instance, would ever have thought of such a hideous idea as child care centers, for instance? It simply would not have occurred to mothers to solve the problem of child care in a way so profoundly unsatisfactory for both children and adults and ultimately for all of society.

Women, if we had felt powerful and had been setting the terms of our own debate, would never have been persuaded by men to accept child care centers as one of our "issues" (nearly all of which men have defined for us). We would have understood that the reason parents cannot care for children is that men's world is organized insanely, from its basic life-negating values out through every aspect of life. We would have begun, as we have, to ask the world-changing questions: what do *we* value? How do we want to live? What kinds of work really need to be done? How many hours a day of work would that take per person? How could we organize society so that everyone's needs could be met, only useful and healthful work would be done, and everyone would have time to live?

I dream of a world in which women are willing to take responsibility for reshaping the world. I dream of a world in which children do not entrust their lives to us only to have us, traitor-like, turn them over to the soul-killing, joy-destroying agents of patriarchy—particularly its schools.

Though the teachers in patriarchy's schools are mostly women, regardless of their bravery and gifts they are fronting unwittingly for the fathers. Daily they enculturate children with patriarchal values and encourage patriarchal thought and behavior. I am not the only mother who has watched and protested futilely in misery and rage while the schools battered her children's psyches and minds. I can't remember why I ever thought I had to send them there.

I ask the young women now having babies everywhere if they are prepared to make a new world for their children. Are they, for instance, prepared to rethink men's competitive, hierarchical, creativity-murdering education altogether?[1] I ask them if they are ready perhaps to get others like themselves together to do *themselves* whatever their children need. Are they ready to go ahead on their own without relying on men's imprimatur or funding?

We are fond of asserting that though men obviously do not care about the well-being of children, fortunately women do. But to the degree that women are not prepared to take full responsibility for creating from the ground up the world their children need, to the degree

[1] Marge Piercy has done a remarkable job of this in *Woman on the Edge of Time*. Ballantine Books: New York, 1976.

that they are still in their dependent, victim, powerless minds, I believe their having children is as immoral as anything men do. Women's passivity is not excused by men's evil. Neither is it less destructive.

I would go farther than asserting the immorality of bringing children into men's child-torturing world. I would say that any conscious woman who bears a child without the intent to structure her child's environment *actively and fully* so that that child cannot be destroyed daily by the fathers is committing a crime against humanity.

It is as reprehensible as it is unnecessary any longer to bring children into the old world. We are capable of doing something completely different and I think we do not need to worry much about what that something is. We can begin by doing *anything* else; anything else will be a sign that we are not morally and spiritually dead, anything else will be an incredible achievement, a massive improvement, a movement toward life and health and a cause for rejoicing.

If we choose to be mothers, we have no choice but to organize our world as it needs to be for mothers and children alike. The most obvious and crucial part of our living in a new, feminist society will be that we make taking women and children seriously our first priority, that we treat them as the sacred, holy ones they are.

CHAPTER 14

The Diabolical Time Clock

With the second half of the Women's Movement in this country—the late 60s, early 70s—the men in control began an all-out siege against women's freedom, a very successful part of which has been their continuing, brilliant "biological-time-clock" campaign. If they could no longer keep us nailed to the system through wifehood, they would step up the never-fail motherhood campaign, knowing that women on their own may be unruly and obstreperous and leave men and threaten patriarchy, but they will be docile and obedient and stay put to keep their children safe.

It seems to me that ever since men took over heaven and earth, no woman has had a free choice to be a mother. If we choose to have children, we cannot know how much we have been affected by brainwashing to do so, we cannot assume that we are the exceptions, the one totally untouched by the massive propaganda campaign to make mother-slaves of us all. If we choose not to have children, we cannot be sure our decision was not made in *reaction* to this terrific coercion.

So whether we decide to be or not to be mothers, neither choice can be said to be made freely. In patriarchy women are not only captives in physical fact, but we are slaves in our beliefs about ourselves, who we are, what we want and need.

Everywhere feminists—married, single, Lesbian—are having babies, each one swearing that hers was a totally free choice. Each one insists that patriarchy's fiercest and most essential of all messages had nothing whatever to do with *her* decision to become a mother.

In addition to my objection to women's passive acceptance of this brutal world for our children, I also object to our hiding from ourselves the dynamics of our conditioning to be mothers and the service we do the state by fulfilling that expectation, obeying that command.

Our work as women, it seems to me, is to stop accepting the male model of motherhood and ourselves make a world in which motherhood is what *we* want and need it to be. If we were to do this, motherhood could become what it has not been for thousands of years—a genuine choice.

I also believe that all of us who are mothers must tell the truth about our experience, first to ourselves, and then to every young unchilded woman who will listen. I am ready now—and without first assuring everyone that I truly love my children so that I won't be stoned to death on the spot—to break this last and deepest of patriarchal taboos by attesting strongly and freely that motherhood was most unsatisfactory for me in this society, as childhood was unsatisfactory for my children, and that, given these conditions, no, I would *not* do it again.

CHAPTER 15

Rearing Nice Sons
Can't Change the World

Many feminists now deciding to have babies are conceiving through artificial insemination. Conception from the most common methods, including the "turkey baster," results in a very high percentage of male births. When I point this out to women who have not yet given birth, they are unconcerned, and when I touch on the problem with women who have already borne sons, they assure me that I needn't worry; they will rear their boys so differently, turn them into such a new breed of men, that the world will be changed.

I'm certain that when they say this they are utterly sincere and well-meaning. I am certain that they have no intention of insulting the vast rest of us—living and dead—who have had sons we were not able to turn into a new breed of men. I'm equally certain they believe *they* will succeed where hundreds of generations of us have failed.

But it still hurts me that they so thoughtlessly participate in this unconscious blaming of all previous mothers for the wretched condition of the world. I am surprised that they believe that women *can* change the basic formative fact of men's lives—which is that every man born automatically has violence-based-and-perpetuated privilege—by rearing their sons to be profeminist.

After long thought, I have concluded that women who have not been the mothers of adolescent males understand neither their own position in patriarchy nor the position of their sons. Patriarchy tells mothers unctuously that we are very important and have much influence, but its behavior speaks louder than these words. Of all persons in patriarchal society, mothers have been set up to have least credibility.

In the face of this enormous handicap, and despite there being at present no way to be a man that is both acceptable to the Mothers as well as to the fathers, we have been able to counter some of what patriarchy has taught our sons about how to be human. And so our sons may be more conscious, less violent, more decent than their forebears (though to counteract feminist influence, male media violence has been stepped up a hundredfold; mothers' love is simply no match for it).

Despite our best efforts, however, our sons *must* be male. And to be male in patriarchy means to have automatic privilege in relation to the females of one's group, privilege one gets *only* through unceasing male violence and terrorism against them. Until this is no longer true, our sons will be characterologically damaged by patriarchy *no matter what we do*. Until this is no longer true, it doesn't matter how hard we try to teach our sons another way of being men, they will in some way still be monsters. Some less monstrous than others, but all monstrous.

This is the reason that women's raising sons has not changed the world, not because mothers didn't want passionately for our sons to be decent, loving, and good, and do everything we could think of to bring that about, but because by its very nature having privilege at others' expense renders one unable to be fully decent, loving, and good.

This is the reason feminists rearing sons can never change the world. We must simply give up forever the idea that we can change anything *through* someone else: our sons, our husbands, any man, any other woman. We can only change ourselves. That's all, but that's the She/Volution.

CHAPTER 16

Hey, You Gynes!

"You guys" is an expression that most of us heard a lot and many of us often used as we were growing up—first in addressing girls as well as boys, and then as we matured, in addressing women as well as men. But upon becoming feminists, as we made a serious effort to clean the sexism out of our language, "you guys" became so thoroughly unacceptable that when it occasionally slipped out of our mouths, we suffered the sort of guilt we had previously reserved for venial sin.

So in this state of precarious grace, we searched for alternatives to "you guys" without noticeable success: you kids, you women, you girls[1]—nothing had a comparably informal, catchy ring.

---

[1] I am completely unpersuaded by the rationalizations in the Movement for calling women "girls."

Until lately. It happened early in the evening of my speech at the University of California in San Diego in January 1989. The women of the Women's Center who had arranged the event took me out to eat. During dinner one of them, trying to get the attention of the group, said loudly, "Hey, *you gynes*, listen a minute!" "That's it!" I crowed, "Perfect!"

It turned out that they too had been having trouble getting "you guys" out of their repertoire, had, in fact, talked about it frequently among themselves. Then finally one of them, in a flash of brilliance, dazzled the group with "you gynes." Her stroke of genius has proved a mighty relief to me. Now I can say what almost comes naturally and still be politically correct.

Other words to designate us still present a problem, however. For instance, like many other feminists, I no longer find the words "woman" and "women" acceptable. But neither do I think variations such as "wimmin" or "womyn" or "womon" are significant improvements. Their attempted disguise of the words "man" and "men" is not complete enough even for written language and is, of course, nonexistent for speech.

For me, the only possible alternative is one that erases all indication of maleness altogether, such as the words "wom" (that I pronounce as in "wom"an) and "wim" in Gerd Brantenberg's delightful book, *Egalia's Daughters*.[2]

Having said this, my continued use of "woman" and

---

[2] Gerd Brantenberg, *Egalia's Daughters*. Seal Press: Seattle, WA, 1985.

"women" in this book is admission that I am compromising my beliefs. Perhaps I rationalize when I say that it seems to me that I must first find the courage when speaking to use "wom" and "wim" exclusively before they will appear as anything but alien to me when I write. My hope is that by the time I write my next book, these or some similar wom-respecting terms will be so familiar to me that they will fairly leap from my pen.

That will be an interesting experiment, using only "wom" and "wim" in my speeches as well as in my daily conversation. But that's what feminism demands—life as experiment.

CHAPTER 17

Gay Rights and AIDS:
Men's Issues
Sidetracking Feminism Again[1]

On October 11, 1987, I was not in the streets of Washington, D.C., marching in the National March for Lesbian and Gay rights. In fact, though I lived only ten minutes from downtown D.C., I refused to go. I refused to go because I refused by my presence to lend credence to the phallacy that gay rights include rights for Lesbians. Gay rights are rights for men. To the degree that they are won, women will find once again that we have drained our vast creative energies into men's lives

---

[1] This piece is abstracted roughly from an interview with me by Cynthia Yockey that was published in the Washington D.C. gay paper, *Lambda Rising Book Report, A Contemporary Review of Gay & Lesbian Literature*, Vol. 1, No. 2, pp. 1 and 5.

only to have little or none of it return to bless us. It is absurd to continue to believe that laws in patriarchy can or will protect women. Because the very foundations of patriarchy rest on our bowed heads and bent backs, men's laws never have protected us and never will.

When we talk about the gay movement, we are in reality talking about two very distinct and disparate movements, as disparate as men's and women's realities in this act of the human drama. It is true that both movements are about rights for men, that people involved in both are under the mistaken assumption that homosexuality is the same phenomenon in women as in men, and that both labor under the even greater misconception that women's and men's experiences in society are alike enough that they can be united fairly by what appears to be a common oppression.

But the similarities stop there. One movement is comprised of the men who are directly affected by whatever gains are made. The other is composed of women who are working for rights for gay men, who naively believe that gay men are our "brothers" and that when they win, we win; women who still need men's approval; women who still need to believe that men care about us as we care about them; women who may be sexual with other women but who are basically male-identified, needing the feeling of importance that associating with the ruling class affords the slaves.

Gay men are men. They may be oppressed in many ways, but because they are male, like their heterosexual brothers they have privilege at the expense of every woman living. Patriarchy is set up for men. It is organized to work to some degree for all men and though obviously less for some than for others, still *exclusively* for men. Though gay men suffer discrimination in comparison with heterosexual men, they have many more opportunities and openings in the world than either Lesbians or heterosexual women. On the whole, they make much more money, they are taken much more seriously, they are listened to with much greater respect and attention, and they enjoy direct access to the resources of this all-male club we call society, as well as to the extremely varied and rich resources of their "little sisters" in the Lesbian sorority.

All the while they are sucking the marrow from our bones, the sap from our veins, at least as many of them hate and fear us—and with as much venom and ugliness—as their more sexually conservative brother vampires.

Just as Lesbians run the risk of working for gay rights only to find that gay men, the beneficiaries, are oblivious to their sacrifice, as, man-like, they maddeningly accept them as their due, in the same way, we can also give much time and compassion and energy to AIDS work to find again that our efforts are taken for granted and, worst of all, that we have no time left for our own work, for women's revolution.

Because history attests that there will always be some urgent reason, such as AIDS, for women to put aside our important concerns, we must insist now on putting our own lives first, we must refuse to get sidetracked again. Abolition sidetracked us, men's wars sidetracked us, the peace movement sidetracked us, Central American politics and the so-called New Age movement have currently united with AIDS to sidetrack us. We can go on forever fighting men's battles.

I am not suggesting that we ignore AIDS or that we be unfeeling about others' lives. But I am suggesting that the vast majority of AIDS victims are men and that men need to learn to take care of themselves and one another. I am suggesting that we stop matronizing gay men and realize that they are grown up and can deal with their own community disaster; that they *need* to deal with it, need to learn whatever it has to teach them, and that we deprive them of this when we rush in to do for them what they should be learning to do for themselves.

Any mother will tell you that if you take over a child's life and deal with his every crisis, you infantilize him, you prevent him from developing the characterological depth, from learning the compassion, from finding the skills he might otherwise have found.

AIDS is horrific; no one deserves it, no one brings it upon themselves. But I think feminists need seriously to consider the possibility that men with AIDS, and gay men without AIDS, and heterosexual men without AIDS, and women who are not feminists and don't identify with women anyway—that these people are the ones who must help the stricken gay community, who must give what needs to be given.

There are so few of us who understand the importance

of women in the world at this time that we must not allow ourselves to forget for a moment the purpose for which we were born, must not allow anyone else's problems to supersede our great work or to distract us from it. We must remain loyal to women, never again to allow ourselves to put women's needs and lives on hold while we take care of *any* men for *any* reason. If we remain at the level of development where any trouble that arises in the men's world can lay first claim to our time and attention, we will not have the integrity, energy, or direction to build a new world, the work we came to Earth to do.

After all, if we don't learn to take women seriously, nobody else is going to either. And the world can no longer survive women's not having a foremost place on it, and in it, and in our hearts.

When women object, "But we don't have horrible problems like AIDS," I have to remind them about women's lives, including the fact that every year men in this country murder 10,000 of us—an FBI figure and therefore ridiculously low. While it is true that in the last three years 24,000 men have died of AIDS, in the same time men have murdered *at least* 30,000 women. We read and hear about AIDS everywhere, but hardly any notice is paid to the terrorist regime under which women survive—unless some man provides a sensation by being electrocuted for murdering more than his share of us.

Women say to me, "But we don't have anything like AIDS" not only because they have been blinded to the danger their own lives are in every second, but also because they have been taught to deny the massive incest and battering and rape and poverty. In particular, they have been trained to deny their spiritual slavery, their lack of belief in themselves and other women and in their importance. Internalized oppression is a far more serious disease than AIDS, afflicting as it does more than half the human race.

Our inability to believe in and love ourselves—that's an AIDS of the soul that's been raging now for 5,000 years and has wiped out millions of women. And we don't have a problem? And we've got to rush out there and help the guys with AIDS? Such behavior is a symptom of our own dis-ease: we will run off at once to attend to the first thing that happens to men and leave women dying, not even seeing them, not even caring because we don't care enough about ourselves.

I have learned all too well how few men—gay or otherwise—want to hear about women's oppression. In order not to have to listen, they often immediately begin to talk about men's problems, tell me that men are oppressed too. The effect is to mask women's oppression or to erase it altogether.

This is easier to understand when it applies to race. White women, for instance, have a decided tendency to display the same behavior with women of color. It is often so painful to hear about our collaboration in their oppression that we say to them, "Well, you know, we've got problems, too. I mean, white middle class women's lives are not all a bed of roses." Their answer to us is the same answer we give the men who complain about their "oppression": "We have been forced to look at you constantly for centuries. By focusing our attention again on *your* experience, you are making *our* experience invisible. If you don't want to know about us, don't listen, but don't ask us to listen to your problems any more. If you want to hear ours, you will have to put yours aside, because ours are very different."

Women's lives and problems are very different from men's, as different as if we fell to earth from the Pleiades, and Lesbian experience is equally alien in comparison with that of gay males.

Perhaps I could find some time in my life for gay men's difficulties if that community were rallying to women's catastrophes, if gay men on a grand scale were demonstrating a keen and urgent understanding of women's torture by pouring money and time and energy and love into the Women's Liberation Movement. Since I see almost no evidence of this, however, I am not in a hurry to donate the precious days of my life to gay men.

CHAPTER 18

She/Volutionizing "Process"'

P rocess figures prominently in feminist parlance these days. A belief in process is both a belief that old habits don't give way easily on this planet yet and an expectation to have to repeat the same new lessons many times before they supplant our former tapes, to have to experience and practice new feelings and behavior many times before they become automatic.

But many of us sigh with impatience even as we think this. We are tired of "process"; we want fiats. We talk about how some day, when we have advanced in our development on this planet, change *will* occur spontaneously. We remind ourselves that if time is not linear, process is an illusion, *must be* an illusion. How, we ponder, can this be made to fit our sense of the reality of process?

I suspect that one difference between process and

193

instantaneous change is that whereas process is along a two-dimensional continuum—from point A to point B—instantaneous change is three- maybe four-dimensional, global: we are *in* the change, we *are* the change, all aspects of the persons and circumstances involved are connected and cross-connected in every possible direction, across planes, through dimensions, not just held together by one tenuous horizontal line.

After a speech in Cincinnati in January 1988, in which I mentioned my preoccupation with this puzzle, the audience and I began discussing the possibilities of instantaneous change. One woman offered the thought that perhaps instantaneous change is a natural law that women once understood and lived in accord with, a law that over the length and increasing depth of our history as slaves we have forgotten.

Later, out in the lobby, another woman proposed a model for independent event versus process: "Think of it this way," she proposed. "A chicken grows inside an egg, finally getting big enough to begin pecking its way out. It pecks and pecks and one day its beak breaks through the shell. That instant, the beak's breaking the shell, is an event, not a process."

This meshed with my perceptions that any point in the sequence of events we call "process" can be viewed as a unique event, that what we call process is the sum of unique events that are connected in ways that are not obvious to us. Perhaps experiencing "process" is strictly a function of perception; perhaps if we weren't thinking in linear-time, cause-and-effect terms, we wouldn't see such occurrences as "process," but would judge each moment alone and as equal with the others, causing change to appear essentially instantaneous.[1]   Janet Blaustein talking about this at Womongathering in Pennsylvania in June 1988 added that because we see linearity in some events and some circumstances, perhaps we pick up the false idea that the linear model is true for or applicable to everything.

In that same lunchtime discussion, I suggested the possibility that each point in our lives can be viewed as an end in itself, as enough, as our having arrived. That is, that perhaps one difference between process and instantaneous change is that there is no goal in the latter model—or that if there is, we reach it every moment.

I remembered something Jane Mara from Seal Rock, Oregon, had told me nearly a year before as we puzzled about this in my kitchen in Virginia, trying to figure out how to *think* about there being no linear time and what that meant about change.

How could one even imagine spontaneous change, given the "reality," for instance, that baby chicks and vegetable seeds have to develop along a time line, have to go through a "process," are apparently caught in linear time?[2]

Mara told me about another woman in Virginia,

---

[1] Conversation with Susan Horwitz, June 1988.

[2] Mara is working on a book, *Emotions: Use and Abuse*. She has been accused of having process as her middle name.

Machaelle Small Wright, who had become acquainted with devas, or nature spirits, at Findhorn in Scotland. Putting her knowledge to work in her own garden in Virginia on her return home, she subsequently wrote a book in which she tells about carrots growing instantaneously from seeds into six-inch plants before her eyes.[3]

Months later, I admitted to Mara on the phone that I was still grappling with the problem of instantaneous change versus process. During that conversation, I tentatively offered the idea that perhaps we go through process because we think process is necessary, the "way things are." Perhaps belief in process *produces* process, and that if we believed in instantaneous change instead, we would get *that*.

She replied that she had not only thought of that already, but that she had become aware that she *chose* process over immediate change, that in fact *her process was resistance to immediate change*. "Instantaneous change is overwhelming, very frightening," she told me, "so I devise a process to take me slowly, to acclimate me to change. For instance, though I'm certain I could do it if I weren't afraid, right now it's too scary for me to zap myself into your kitchen, to find myself suddenly there in your house with you. I think I may opt for the process of *getting* there instead of just *being* there because otherwise I would discover how powerful I really am. That discovery would obligate me to change my whole life, it

---

[3] Machaelle Small Wright, *Behaving as if the God in All Life Mattered.* Perelandra: Jeffersonton, VA, 1987, pp. 119-120.

would put incredible responsibility upon me that I don't feel ready to accept. So I take the plane, I take the safe, comfortable, powerless way out, I make small 'reasonable' demands upon myself, out of fear I remain blind to myself, to my potentialities, my capacities."

If it is true for the rest of us that our process, like Mara's, is resistance to instantaneous change—and I think this is probable—then like her we are all likely to hold on to process until we become braver, until we dare experiment with the frightening possibilities a little at a time and a little at a time face the implications of the fact that we can change reality with incredible rapidity—instantaneously.

Perhaps in an already overwhelmingly complex sensory world, and one with the potential of infinitely greater complexity, we also choose process because it orders and categorizes experience, because it simplifies, because it reduces ambiguity and tension. Clearly, without our silent agreement with one another and with the universe to follow certain principles of organization, life might be inordinately confusing.

But also fascinating. Personally, I am becoming bored and very impatient with the restrictions I daily impose upon myself—believing I must pick up the telephone to communicate with someone at a distance, for example.

The use of technology best illustrates our firm belief in process, the belief that we need some intermediary—such as a telephone, an airplane, a computer—to do the things that we could do far quicker and more efficiently ourselves.[4] If we altered our profound belief that we need such technology, such clumsy, slow, imperfect, limited intermediaries, alternatives would have the space and the energy and the permission to appear to us. I believe we must begin to believe in our unaided selves in order for those selves to reveal to us their stupendous powers.

Peace Pilgrim made such a discovery for herself years ago when she first began walking for peace. For the first few years she wore only a scarf and sweater in the winter, and then discarded even them as unnecessary. She writes, "I'm now so adjusted to changes in temperature that I wear the same clothes summer and winter, indoors and out." [5] Apparently, this is common practice in less technologically-minded, less left-brained societies, such as exist, for example, in Tibet and Nepal. That this is obviously possible opens the mind to the existence of all kinds of amazing possibilities.

I am preparing myself for what is commonly thought impossible, knowing that impossibility is created by disbelief. I am getting ready for anything, everything, am open to any possibility. I accept that anything I can imagine is possible; more than that, that my thinking it, my believing it, *creates* the possibility of it.

---

[4] Conversation with Susan Horwitz, February 1989.

[5] *Peace Pilgrim: Her Life and Work in Her Own Words.* Ocean Tree Books: Santa Fe, NM, 1982, p. 56.

But I also accept that I can never imagine freely, wildly enough to reach the limits of possibility. We have, for example, hardly begun to imagine, to say nothing of to invent, the world that many of us will live to see.

CHAPTER 19

Escape from the Semi/Versity[1]

Not long ago at the reception following my speech at a midwestern university, six or seven instructors from the Women's Studies Department stayed at the reception afterward until everyone else had gone. Then with tense, anxious faces they told me that they were miserable in their profession. They were realizing that they had edited themselves so severely in their teaching and scholarship—and often so unconsciously—that they had forgotten what they had once thought. They also saw that now they would never know how spiritually and intellectually high they might have soared if they had not

---

[1] Wilma Scott Heide, *Feminism for the Health of It*. Margaretdaughters, Inc: Buffalo, NY, 1985, p. 4: "There is no university in the sense of universal truth. There are only semiversities of essentially white, heterosexual, androcentric thought patterns."

been pinned to the ground by fear for their jobs. They were frightened by how insidiously they had slipped into compromising their principles and mourned the courage they had lost through accommodation.

Though each of them was totally dedicated to teaching women about their history, to illuminating women's position and the reasons for it, and to helping women discover their own power, they could hardly face going to work another day. Several of them stated unequivocally that they wanted to leave. They felt as if they had to or they would lose their moral bearings altogether. They would do it in a minute, they vowed, if they weren't so afraid of "economics."

Though as fed up as the others, one of them tried to persuade them that it was their duty to stick it out. "The women here *need* us," she pleaded with them. "For most of them, there's no other place to learn about themselves as women. But what's more important, they need us as *models*."

"But what are you modeling for them?" I asked. "Do you really think they need more models of women compromising their principles, sacrificing their integrity either for money or for what they perceive as others' needs? Women who are saying less, being less, muting and scaling themselves down, bowing to the yoke? I should think they have had enough of such models."

I asked them how they thought they could help other women find their sources of personal power when they themselves felt so powerless and thought so little of themselves that they accepted and played men's hierarchical, competitive game even though they knew it was in gross violation of all they valued. I told them I would have thought that instead their women students most desperately needed models of women having integrity, valuing their own women's culture, acting powerful and fearless, being free.

As we spoke together, I questioned whether it was even possible for women to glimpse our own real power and potential in universities where we are forced to conform to the rules and values patriarchy deliberately set up to keep women from having access to our Selves. If the means are the ends, surely this is impossible.

They asked what I would do if I were in their shoes. I replied that since I wasn't, I couldn't know, but that I trusted them to figure it out. To begin to open their minds to the possibilities, I told them a story I had heard about a group of women like them who, in the early 70s, had left their university positions and organized themselves to teach women's studies in the community. The story goes that they were successful enough to continue for at least a half dozen years.

Though perhaps apocryphal, this story is nevertheless absolutely true *in its possibility*. It *could* very well have happened, and could happen, or happen again, at any time. Individual women have done it—Kay Hagan in Atlanta, for example. Why couldn't a group of women set themselves up to teach women's studies in every community, perhaps naming it something more compelling—Kay calls hers "Feminars"—and teach *everything* they ever longed to teach in exactly the way they always longed to teach it? Not a "feminist university"—which seems to me an oxymoron, like military intelligence—but a whole new concept.

But, the argument against this goes (and you can probably hear it in your own head right now), no one would take such classes seriously because they wouldn't be recognized in the men's world, and men wouldn't award them "credits" toward "degrees."

The question this raises is obvious: why should we be, why *are* we, interested in being recognized by men? Why are we interested in their "degrees?" The answers bring us full circle: because we need men's imprimatur in order to get jobs teaching subjects such as women's studies in universities, or working in other patriarchal prisons.

Everywhere I go in the United States I find young women working toward degrees and older women returning to school for degrees. Though it is true that success in school gives women's confidence a sturdy boost, it is *not* true that it necessarily improves their economic situation. In Ohio, for instance, the average yearly income for college-educated women is $10,000— an income that can barely support life, to say nothing of assuring that life of some reasonable quality. Older women, of course, fare worst.

Even if a woman has a doctorate and obtains a teaching position at a university, she will find no job security there. Until she gets locked into the tenure cell, she is usually at the mercy of yearly contract renewals that all too often do not come through—a terrorist tactic, one of men's cruelest ways of controlling our lives. In

California as well as in other states, this has made women university teachers the new Okies—itinerant, rootless, securityless, devalued, underpaid. University education is not working economically for women. Nothing is.

Some may ask, if women could have abundance without recourse to prostitution in the universities or in any of patriarchy's other garrisons, what evidence do we have that even then they would choose to give up the prestige dependent upon hierarchy and male approval? What evidence is there that such women do not so completely depend for their identity and sense of importance on patriarchy, are not so thoroughly co-opted morally and psychically, that they would actually choose peerness and integrity instead? Is there evidence that they would give up their privileged-prisoner rights for freedom?

If we look with the expectation of seeing it, perhaps there is more evidence that they would than we might at first think. Those women in that midwestern university *do* exist. They *do* know that they are servants of a system that survives only by destroying women, and they *are* suffering consciously from this knowledge.

Others like them *must* exist in every brainwashing, destructive institution of the fathers: businesses and corporations, schools, churches, legislatures, courts, and governments. Enough of them may have the courage to get up off their knees and deal on their own terms directly with other women. Especially if some of these other women are already busy creating a literal new society in which no woman needs to sell her soul to survive.

But (the argument about women's leaving the universities continues) women don't take women seriously. We particularly don't take seriously women acting without men's stamp of approval in ways that radically undermine male domination. So who is to say that women who escape from the universities and strip away their titles to engage in truly feminist learning experiments in daring new ways will attract anyone to participate with them?

No one can know for sure, of course. But so many women are so fed up with the dim little half-lives they are allowed, even compelled, to live, that if any other possibility presented itself with courage and passion, I have faith that, to save their lives, they would choose to join those of us who were intent on carrying it forward.

To attract participants, the prisoners of war who had so bravely escaped would have to make their prison break widely known. Potential collaborators would have to find out that a new prospect for women had now opened up. They would have to read persuasive notices, articles, and flyers describing and inviting in ways that made them feel valiant and proud. They would have to see a wide range of ideas offered for discussion, most of which university dons would not only never officially sanction but at their mere suggestion would wet their trousers. They would have to be assured that the escapees were not merely duplicating the male system. They would, that is, have to know that there would be no hierarchy, no titles, no competition, no grades, no condescension. And that there would be an honest search for a new and more valid form of female achievement than "male scholarshit." [2] Prospective participants would have to be persuaded that the objective genuinely was freedom and that it was being pursued with utmost boldness.

But most of all, word would have to get out that this experiment was changing women radically. If through these classes, women were able to leave behind their terror of men and men's approval, divesting themselves of the patriarchal claptrap that had previously determined their nearly every thought and feeling; if they came to think with outrageous nonconventionality, learning to love women and to take our ways seriously; if, inspired to view themselves as actors on a cosmic stage, they changed the structure and substance of their lives in large and stunning ways—then the renegade "women's studies" teachers would know they were creating the kind of model women genuinely need, a feminist model of integrity, self-esteem, autonomy, and power.

And then in a moonlit ceremony, with the blessing of the wind and sky we could pronounce them all wild women. They could pronounce themselves a new species: *free women.*

---

[2] As Marlene Mountain from Hampton, Tennessee so aptly describes it. This reminds me of a slip an acquaintance made in my home one night as she fervently described an authority figure in her life as "one of the world's foremost biblical *squalors!*"

Part III

WOMEN'S ABUNDANT UNIVERSE

Preface to Part III

I had finished this book and sent it in to the publishing firm that was originally scheduled to publish it. It had been edited and was ready for my final corrections before being sent to the typesetter. Though I felt vaguely dissatisfied with the last Part, I couldn't pinpoint what was wrong. So I shrugged and gave up. I had done my best.

The last chapter contained several examples of community projects women are working on in this country. None of these was perfect, of course, but then, I rationalized, we are in a peculiar time, an interim space—one foot in and one foot out of patriarchy.

Then as I was doing a final check of information, a woman whose project I had described at length mentioned that she was still searching for funding. Somehow this coalesced my reasons for discontent with the chapter. I knew at that moment that most of the material I had included in it did not belong in this book, and I knew why.

First, my motive was wrong. I was giving in to the pressure to "give examples" of what might "really" be done, trying to alleviate the anxiety that is natural to the terrific ambiguity of being feminists at this moment in time. Ambiguity should not be dispelled even if it could be. It is necessary.

Second, in giving examples I limited the possibilities. None of them was an example of a genuinely new mode, a distinctly different order. All of them were variations on women's age-old accommodation theme—how we can live easier *in patriarchy*, how we can get the system to work a little better for us.

Third and most important, I had not thought wildly enough myself. Specifically, I had not dared out into the wilderness beyond the bounds of money. The moment I knew, however, that I had to discard the whole last Part as it then existed, I knew what had to take its place. I had to examine the blocks money sets up in our minds and in the ecosystem before I could see how we could reestablish the flow of energy in our lives and in the life of the planet. In Chapter 20 I had mentioned Genevieve Vaughan's work on this subject. Now I knew that I had to do more than mention it; I had to make it the basis of the entire section.

As usual, it had taken my mind a couple of months to digest, understand, and bring to consciousness the significance of an idea that was destined to change my life.

What follows, then, is the best gift I can give at this time toward recreating women's abundant universe.

CHAPTER 20

Lilies of the Field

I chanced one day upon what may have been the world women knew before patriarchy, that world of wholeness and unity so lost to us. One glorious spring day while I was still a Mormon wife and mother and a baby feminist, I was driving down a road in rural Virginia on my way to the supermarket. The closed car began to grow uncomfortably warm with the bright sun beating upon it, so I turned my attention to rolling down the window.

As I did, I suddenly realized that through that opening window I was not merely looking at but was caught up in and participating with a breathtaking world. Now, a dozen years later, I remember best the woods that were ablaze with a green so intense that like a leafy wildfire it sprang through my eyes into my body and burned along every nerve and bone and muscle until I felt as if I *were* its green-hot glow.

Totally part of that dazzling world for a few seconds, I felt released from time. Whether the whole experience lasted a century or a split second was irrelevant; the conventional designations were meaningless. The time-lessness affected me strongly, though, and unexpectedly. In it I felt whole and large and real, very deep and rich. I awed myself and was awed by everything around me. I wanted to laugh and clap my hands for joy. I wanted to weep. I wanted to remain the rest of my life in that state of complete knowledge of myself and of intimate, loving participation with the earth. I knew for those few moments that if I could figure out how to do it, this was fully possible.

If the scrim between me and the world as it truly is and can be is able to part for one magical moment to let me experience again a little of what is possible for human consciousness, my assumption is that it parts for others, too. So perhaps many of us know absolutely to what dim and muffled numbness patriarchy has reduced our senses and our minds, and something of what the "real" world is like.

That blazing green, timeless forest is one of my touch-stones. Recollecting it, I am reminded of the possibilities for my life. It buttresses the other reference points that over the years have verified for me that joy, actual and readily available, is my human legacy. It fills me with incentive and hope, infuses me with energy and purpose. Who would choose to suffer in patriarchy if they under-stood that right at hand, all around us where we stand, a wondrous world *already exists* for us to step into and make our own?

Sometimes I think that we need not worry about creating a world at all but only about recreating ourselves so that the world that is there, that is in us, that *is* us, can become our external, concrete reality. I also know that as a universal gender class we have already moved into a different spiritual dimension, onto our own unique moral plane. Despite how crucial our inner transformation is, however, I know that it must manifest itself in some integral, external activity.

What that activity might be is becoming clearer. Thousands of us now believe that we have no choice but to build together an actual, physical society to our own specifications. Prime among these specifications is that each one of us has enough of what we need to live; specifically, as in the archaic world, plenty of *time*.

To establish hierarchy, the antithesis of women's world order, patriarchy had to create scarcity—of respect, of honor, of food and other essentials, but primarily of time.

All around me every day I hear people complain, "I don't have time." "There's not enough time." "I need 36 hours in every day." I say it myself, although I know that there is plenty of time, all the time we could possibly ever need; time is what there is an infinite supply of in the universe, and time is life. Perhaps we should ask ourselves the obvious question, "If there is plenty of time and *I* don't have it, where is it, who has it, and how can I get my share of it back?"

That this scarcity of time has seemed inevitable until now is instructive. If you can persuade people that there isn't enough time, if you can persuade them that this time deprivation is unchangeable "reality," and if you can simultaneously organize society in a way that bears out your contention that there seems in fact to be very little time, you can steal people's lives from them.

The initial time/life you would steal would be from their *minds*. Your success in getting people to *think* there is no time would cause them to limit themselves. By causing them to behave *as if it were true,* you could effectively establish time-poverty as their reality.

What would happen to tyrants if slaves refused the concept of limited time? What if they believed that there was all the time they needed, and freely partook of it to think, to talk and listen to one another, to dream, to love fully, to create music, art, and literature, to play games and climb mountains? What would happen to tyranny if slaves had time? Tyranny, nonfreedom, means primarily having no time for oneself. Ownership of others' bodies means dictating how those bodies spend their *time*.

When I hear everyone moaning that they have no time, I am made freshly aware of how patriarchy tyrannizes us all by taking from us our time. Free people need not only space—rooms of their own—but time of their own as well. Any beneficent[1] society, therefore, that is not simply the old one under a different rubric must first free our time, give us "free time." That such an expression as "free time" exists is evidence that the rest of our time is "slave time."

Thinking about the necessity of time deprivation to patriarchy led me to examine the underlying assumptions that we must accept in order to participate in the delusions, the absurd beliefs, that only brainwashing could have made appear reasonable.

One of these is that we must spend most of our precious time/life working. Not only that we must do this in order to live, but that as men have narrowly defined it—whether enjoyable or not, whether mind- or spirit-expanding or not—work has been made to seem desirable in itself. We have been programmed to consider ourselves "good" if we work and "bad" if we don't. Our strong work enculturation teaches us that if we are not working—which usually means producing something saleable or in some way facilitating the movement of money through society—we are idle, not doing anything of value, and are worthless, good-for-nothing parasites. We have also been strongly indoctrinated to consider

---

[1] When Susan Horwitz pointed out to me that the word "alternative" is a relational, comparative word, I realized that as such it is always on the one-down side of the dichotomy that comparison establishes. An "alternative society," therefore, is perceived as smaller, less powerful, and less important than the one with which it is being compared. Susan added that according to what I say in this chapter, *patriarchy* is the "alternative society." This is the reason I do not speak of women's world as an "alternative."

work done for payment superior to that done freely.

But what if we stopped believing the calculated non-sense that each of us has to work eight or more hours a day simply to survive? Think what we could be and do! What would we do if we didn't feel hurried, if we didn't suffer from chronic time-panic? What would we do if we had endless hours of freedom stretching out before us as far as we could see?

It seems to me that we might come to know ourselves and one another. We might relax into a deep connection with our own planet and the multitudes of other stars in our galaxy. We might begin to move to rhythms long since muted by hurry-scurry.

I believe that reframing our concept of time, diminishing it to a straight line between two points, and then goading us mercilessly along it has been one of patriarchy's most substantial successes. This revolution in the concept of time was absolutely necessary for patriarchy to gain a hold on the human mind and thence on the world. I am certain that it remains essential to retaining control of the planet and its inhabitants. As long as we live our daily lives according to unexamined patriarchal assumptions about time, we are at the mercy of the cruelest taskmaster of all the fathers, "Father time."

"Father time" forces us to live each day within such strict brackets that most of what is desirable and possible in life is outside them. Lashing our psyches with his whip, he maintains the necessary lie that we have no time for and therefore can't do most of the things we genuinely *want* to do. At the same time, his terrorism keeps our creativity so suppressed that we can barely imagine what we *would* do if we had time. It keeps us so automatized that we seldom even think to question his twin assertions that time is scarce and that we have no choice but to use up the little we have of it slaving to maintain the patriarchal state.

"I don't have time" is the single most frequently given reason for living fractional, perpetually indentured lives, for not living fully or freely. Because time is life, when we say we don't have enough time, we are admitting that we don't have enough life.

Even the little time we *do* have is Father time, frozen time, dead time, rigidly, obdurately linear time, adamantly cause-and-effectful, swift, superficial, and anxiety-producing, like walking an unraveling tightrope high above the ground.

The assumption enforced by Father time's whip is that time is an external given to which we must adjust our collective and individual pace. But I am beginning to believe rather that time is within us and therefore controllable by each one of us.

In an earlier chapter, I spoke of time as surrounding us, as the element in which we live, as the ocean surrounds fish and is their element. Now I think that perhaps instead each of us swims in our own personal, internal ocean of time rather than in a communal bath. If this is true, then time literally *is* life and life is time, and both are ours to do with as we wish. On the other hand, if we conceive of time as the ocean in which we all swim together, then it is not under each individual's control and

219

goes on whether any one of lives in it or not. This latter way of thinking about time not only contributes to our general feeling of powerlessness in the universe, but by making life dependent upon time but not time upon life, blurs the fact that for each living person time and life are indissolubly merged.

Understanding that time and life are one is particularly essential as a starting point in uprooting the wrong-headed and calamitous exchange economy patriarchy has so carefully taught us to believe is inescapable. In the Western world we often hear the phrase "Time is money," and every successfully socialized adult knows that this is not meant metaphorically but literally. We blur any distinction between time and money thoroughly and unconsciously every time we talk about "spending time," or deplore what certain activities "cost" us in time, or always try to "save" time, or "give" time in the place of money to charities or volunteer organizations, or when we pay a fine with money rather than with time in jail.

If time and life are in many critical ways synonymous, and if in patriarchy time really *is* money, then it follows that on planet Earth money is life.

This, of course, is not news. On many levels we've known it for a very long time. We would have had to be insentient to have missed the connection, living as we do in a world where people literally cannot live now without money, a world where millions of moneyless people are doomed to certain death and the rest of us to lives restricted in direct proportion to our access to money.

In fact, because we believe that money is necessary

for life and have been so terrorized for so long by the chronic lack of it, it is the one assumption of the considerable battery of assumptions the fathers' term "reality" that is most frightening for us to face and difficult to challenge dispassionately. More than any other, it has the power to defeat women's deprogramming methods. Though many of us have known with certainty for some time that everything men have taught us about the world is either wrong or a deliberate lie, in the past not only I but obviously other feminists have not dared to extrapolate from this that money must be tossed out with men's other dangerous nonsense.

But that doesn't mean I have felt comfortable about my cowardice. Women have been saying to me for a long time, "I can't stand to work in patriarchy every day; it's killing me." They have been terrorized by money scarcity for so long that when I suggest that since patriarchy is killing us we should flee from it and try our hand at society-making, almost always their first questions come out of the mind that equates life and money: "But how will we make money? How will we *live*? How will we earn a living?"

Though I have always understood and even shared their fear, I have known that that question sidestepped the difficult-to-believe possibility that no woman needs to work in the patriarchal system if she does not wish to. I have become progressively more convinced that believing in the actuality of our desires is necessary for them to appear. So I choose to believe that neither I nor any woman has to work in patriarchy in order to live, and that

221

our conviction that we do is part of the brainwashing that keeps us imprisoned there.

That question also prompts me to make clear that I am determined to live in a reality in which the concept of "earning" a living seems as bizarre and sad to everyone as it has come to seem to me. The language of that phrase reveals our programming to perceive ourselves as inherently worthless and consequently to accept work as a rational and even welcome atonement for some imagined inadequacy. From that language the irony is evident: by making us perceive success at work as proof of our value, patriarchy tricks us into working long, hard hours to maintain it as a system.

But more than that, that phrase exposes the fathers' cruel lie that we must earn the right to live. Though the fathers have got away with their deception for centuries, the mothers know that at birth life is a free gift of the universe. We know that life doesn't need to be—in fact, *can't* be—earned, and we are destined to recreate that reality.

Like the birds of the air and the lilies of the field, we do not need to toil to be allowed to live.[2] In living out their lives as they wish, they faithfully abet the cycles and flow of all life, scattering seeds, controlling pests, providing beauty, enriching the soil and holding it together,

---

[2] Even most nonreligious, nonchristian readers recognize this allusion to patriarchal literature. Despite its inclusion in men's bible, however, this image is so beautiful and apt that I suspect it of being a remnant and of having its origins in goddess culture.

perfuming the air, providing materials—such as pollen—
that enable other creatures to live in their appointed ways,
in their turn becoming food for others and ultimately for
the soil.

Though the birds and flowers, the fauna and flora,
contribute a great deal and are indispensable members of
the world community, they do not "toil." With them as
our model—though ultimately we may be less essential—
perhaps we can begin to trust that if each of us does what
gives us pleasure and what we do well, if each of us
follows our natural bent and honors it, we too will
enhance the flow of life, facilitate its cycles, meet all
human needs, and have all that we ourselves require.

Though I struggled with it womanfully, I wasn't able
in the past to answer the question, "How shall we earn a
living?" no matter how often or how urgently it was put
to me. After listing my objections to it, however, I finally realized why neither I nor any other feminist could
answer it. Not because we weren't smart enough—we
were twice as smart as we had ever been, thinking at last
both with our heads and our intuitions—but because it
was once again the wrong question.

The right questions do not ask how we can be more
comfortable in patriarchy. They do not seek to discover
how we can "pass." Knowing this, I realized that some-
day I would have to ask what were for me certainly some
of the right questions: what *is* money? Is it necessary? If
not, what else is possible? How might I begin to live in
a moneyless world?

But I wasn't ready to ask them then because I wasn't

ready for the answers. Once answers come, if I wish to be a woman of integrity, I have no choice but to act on them, and I was afraid. The shift from money-thinking and money-fear had to take place first in my mind. Further than that, I had also to stop believing that exchange itself was the only or even the best path to survival.

A handful of feminists has understood from the beginning that money and the philosophy underlying and sustaining it are profoundly patriarchal and therefore inimical to all they valued. I'm certain they have attempted to rid their lives of these most blatant evidences of the workings of the male value system. But I have not asked them about their experiment because until recently my fear caused me to regard these women as rash and uncredible and to dismiss them summarily.

But in the few months that I was finishing this book and sifting down through layer after layer of my brainwashing residue, my flinty refusal to examine my assumptions about money continually impeded my progress. I sabotaged my work not only by ignoring these looming assumptions but also by not recognizing money, price, and related concepts as patriarchal artifacts that prevented my personal liberation.

Though I believe that change must always take place first on the metaphysical level, I also think we are required to study whatever physical alternatives we can find. Following this plan when I ran for President in 1984, I did a crash course in economics during which, to my delight, I discovered Hazel Henderson, a self-taught economist and advisor to heads of state the world over. Her book, *The Politics of The Solar Age: Alternatives to Economics*,[3] is the best readily-available initial deprogramming about patriarchal economics that I know.[4]

In this book she asserts that there is no such thing as economics; *there are only values.* As I read that, I knew she was right. But how did this simple fact become so obfuscated? How did "economics" grow so arcane that it slipped out of our individual control, leaving us at the mercy of others?

Henderson offers one clue. She maintains that economists, eager to be viewed as belonging to the scientific community—so important for men—first invented and then ghettoized economics. By mystifying it they made themselves indispensable as experts to explain it to the

---

[3] Hazel Henderson, *The Politics of the Solar Age: Alternatives to Economics.* Anchor Press/Doubleday: Garden City, NY, 1981.

[4] Women's books on economics have been published before and after hers. All of them that I have been able to find, however, no matter how radical they purport to be, assume the old assumptions—such as that women's work must be included in the Gross National Product, for instance, so we can influence public policy decisions—a level of analysis and inquiry depressingly superficial and conventional. None of them asks basic, assumption-shattering questions such as: why should we accept men's global economic system at all? Why do we think women are powerless to replace it with a way of meeting needs that is completely workable and self-regulating, as well as beneficial for all living things? Are fiscal decisions the really important decisions of this age? Can women create anything new by focusing on the old—pandering to it, struggling for acceptance by it? Most of these authors, by failing to scrutinize the assumptions upon which venerable institutions rest, accept as inescapable much nonsense and evil.

rest of us,[5] and also put themselves in a position to control and manipulate us.

This behavior is so typical of patriarchy that it should elicit no more than a "ho hum" from feminists, a bored "What else is new?" It is so like the fathers to send up continually larger and denser smokescreens to shield their most vulnerable flanks. And "economics" is one of their weakest. Imagine if dreaded "economics," instead of appearing frighteningly complicated and beyond the grasp of most of us, were understood to be merely values. Recognized as eminently mutable—*and by us*—it could no longer reduce us all to powerless pulp.

For this to happen, we would first have to lose our respect and fear of it and our belief that "economics" really *means* something, that it really *describes* something necessary and useful, that it has the capacity to teach us something true about the world. Second, having become totally unimpressed and even a little embarrassed that we had ever perceived it as anything other than patriarchy's ugly values in drag, we would be ready to get rid of men's "economics" by substituting women's "economics"—women's values.

Henderson foresees this, positing "the coming era of posteconomic policy making." "From now on," she writes, "as the economic and price-system levers become ever more divorced from reality, industrial societies will need to refocus their attention on policy levers that are

---

[5] Hazel Henderson, *The Politics of the Solar Age: Alternatives to Economics*, p. 8.

nonmonetary, nonfiscal, and nonprice-oriented." [6]

This is where women come in, this is where we are the gifted, the geniuses—in *value*-based decisions; that is, in decisions that are nonmonetary, nonfiscal, and nonprice-oriented.

Although men have increasingly used economics to terrorize women (and one another), it is equally true that their "economy" is doomed. Soon everyone who is not already doing so will have to rethink radically the ways we live and work together.

Henderson's demystification helped me begin this rethinking by releasing me from much of my anxiety about "economics." But it took another woman's courageous departure from herd-mentality to enable me to understand *how* women can create our own "economy," *how* we can substitute our values for patriarchal values in actual, physical ways in our lives and in the world. Because of her thinking, I was finally able to leap over the barrier and erase money and all exchange dogma from my vision of women's world.

Genevieve Vaughan has a brave and original mind. Her papers, "The Philosophy Behind Stonehaven (An Attempt to Preach What We Practice)," and "Gift Giving:

[6] Hazel Henderson, *The Politics of the Solar Age: Alternatives to Economics*, p. 31.

The Feminine Principle of Communication," [7] advocate a nonmonetary, nonexchange economic model so simple, so evocative of our own personal power, and so in harmony with every idea I had laboriously come to in the past few years, that as I read it, I thought with profound relief, "Of course."

Briefly, Vaughan suggests that the surest escape from the economic scarcity and terror necessary to patriarchy lies in the overt establishment of a gift-giving society. She maintains that such a society already flourishes worldwide in the form of women's free nurturance— flourishes that is, as a *covert* system. [8]

To make certain that this female economic order *remains* covert and invisible, patriarchy overvalues paid labor and assigns status to people and things on the basis of monetary worth. [9] Men's economic philosophy and behavior is in this way the antithesis of and thoroughly reactive to women's values—a fact that helps to explain its devastating effect on the planet and its inhabitants. Reaction is based in fear, and fear, unable to produce

[7] Unpublished manuscripts, 1987 and 1983. Though much of what follows is based on Vaughan's ideas, I take full responsibility for the choice of language. Unless quoted, these are not Vaughan's words or her style of expression. I have fit her material into my own idiosyncratic radical feminist world view.

[8] Genevieve Vaughan, "The Philosophy Behind Stonehaven (An Attempt to Preach What We Practice)," p. 3.

[9] Conversation between Genevieve Vaughan and Susan Horwitz, March 1989.

anything but more of itself, has spawned a fearful, terrifying reality.

Convinced that men's exchange economy is an aberration in human interaction (and a recent one at that), Vaughan holds that the very idea of exchange, including barter, is based on invented rather than on real need—"a manipulated use of need satisfaction," as she puts it. It is also completely conditional: I will only give to you if you give back to me in exact measure. Extending this idea, she maintains that because the values underlying exchange—competition, manipulation, exploitation, justice, and self-aggrandizement—are inherently patriarchal (i.e., hierarchical and oppressive), exchange inevitably produces scarcity, violence, and death.[10]

Mary Ann Beall, another creative thinker, interprets and expands upon Vaughan's work. In her opinion, women's model of society is a replication of the global ecosystem of Earth. Specifically, this means that, understanding the interconnectedness of all things, women cherish, preserve, and facilitate the flow of energy from one life form to another.

We instinctively know—in our viscera, that is—that in damming up that flow and creating surpluses for the benefit of the few, the possibilities for interacting with its life-giving elements are destroyed for the many.[11]

---

[10] Conversations between Genevieve Vaughan and Susan Horwitz, and between Genevieve Vaughan and Sonia Johnson, March 1989.

[11] Conversation with Mary Ann Beall, March 1989.

Beall gives the example of the Aswan dam which was designed to block the River Nile's flow so that cotton and other cash crops could be grown in hitherto unarable soil. In addition to decreasing the size and fertility of the delta, and spreading disease, this blockage stopped the flow of nutriments from the upper Nile that fed the aquatic and other life of the Mediterranean Sea, catastrophically disrupting the food chain for all living things in that area. In their blindness to the intertwining networks that support and sustain all life, men continually and with devastating effect block the ecosystem's energy flow.[12]

Men's economy is designed on this same model—the blockage system of surpluses and dearths in which surpluses are not recycled into the flow. As the adage puts it "stealing from Peter to pay Paul." But systems, including economic systems, are living things, and all living things need flow for survival, they all require the continual movement and recycling of energy. Instead, what we see on the planet today is that all men's systems—capitalism, communism, socialism—are energy dams in multiple ways, drastically interrupting the natural order of things and causing calamities. They can no more succeed for humankind than can the Aswan Dam.

Neither the natural nor the "economic" ecosystem can long sustain the effects of the dams men have built across every living river, physical and metaphysical. Because strife is a major characteristic of blocked flow and

---

[12] Conversation with Mary Ann Beall, March 1989.

violence the inevitable result of a dysfunctional system,[13] we could say that war is a state of advanced global arteriosclerosis.

Money is the congealed energy that clogs society's arteries. In creating it as a symbol of the transformative powers of both physical and spiritual ecosystems, men lost track of what it stood for, where the source of its value originally lay. When they no longer paid attention to the real things that money symbolized, money itself became "real." It took on a life of its own and began to have value in and of itself. In this way men disconnected money from the ecosystem that once generated its value, a disastrous move.[14]

The trouble is, of course, that money is *not* the energy it once symbolized. It is not a member of a community that provides natural checks and balances, give and take. Unlike living things in a healthy life web, it has no internally disciplined flow. It accumulates in piles here and there at the same time that it is almost totally absent from vast areas. Having no inherent life force, like a vampire it can live only on stolen energy.

By cutting down the Amazon forests, for example, men are destroying something inherently valuable to the maintenance of the planet's energy network, and turning it into a pot of money. What they are left with is a pot of money and a barren, wasted land. This is the kind of

---

[13] Conversation with Mary Ann Beall, March 1989.

[14] Conversation with Mary Ann Beall, March 1989.

exchange that is necessary in order to energize money.

Money, or any other medium of exchange, is simply another artifact of the patriarchal mind and more evidence of the deadliness of its values. It is, among other things, the concrete manifestation of the ubiquitous, thoroughly iniquitous, and deeply entrenched belief that inequitable distribution—hierarchy—is unavoidable and even desirable. By forcing everyone constantly to compare the noncomparable—values, objects, ideas, people—on the basis of criteria established by external judges, it encourages the hierarchical, dichotomous mind. In this way, exchange crawls off the same dungheap of values as "an eye for an eye and a tooth for a tooth," the dungheap where reciprocation, comparison, retaliation, greed, and control sit enthroned side by side.

From this and from all else that we know and intuit about men's dammed economy, most of us would conclude, as Vaughan does, that any biophilic way of filling the needs of humans and other living things (i.e., any genuinely workable economy) must be based on such radically different values from those of exchange that exchange drops out of the human economic repertoire altogether.[15]

We would also agree that such an economy or value system has already originated with women. Women's economic answer to exchange—nonreciprocal, non-adversarial gift giving—is based on our foremost value,

[15] Conversation between Genevieve Vaughan and Susan Horwitz, February 1989.

a value that does not even exist in patriarchy: that the needs of living beings and our life systems be met.

Vaughan contends that if women were to behave in the way most comfortable for us and most supportive of our integrity, we would give freely without requiring repayment, establishing gift giving as the exclusive mode of satisfying human needs. In addition, if we had our preference we would assume and expect that because others shared our values and would respond in the same reasonable way, our own needs would also always be met.[16] We would trust in the deep instinct of living things to maintain their delicate, powerful, generative networks.

Strong evidence for this as a probable scenario is that it is the way women have traditionally interacted—though admittedly often one-sidedly—with others and with the earth.[17]

It could be argued, of course, that gift-giving behavior is not necessarily "natural" for women but instead that men, who benefit most from our habit of lavish sharing of our resources, have craftily programmed it into us. Insofar as women have capitulated to men's brainwashing to be selfless and subservient, this is no doubt true. But the likelihood is that men, as is their historically uncreative wont, have in their subjugation of women again merely seized the main chance. This was—and

[16] Genevieve Vaughan, "The Philosophy Behind Stonehaven (An Attempt to Preach What We Practice)," p. 5.

[17] Genevieve Vaughan, "The Philosophy Behind Stonehaven (An Attempt to Preach What We Practice)," p. 2.

is—to capitalize upon and exploit for their own nefarious purposes women's already existing, ancient, aboriginal altruism, communitarianism, and predilection for anarchy, as well as our sense of deep and immediate spiritual interconnectedness with and attitude of responsibility for all other life.

There are those who insist that women are no more generous or life-loving than men. But such persons cannot have looked around them with open eyes. In most households of the world women work daily from dawn to late night attending to the physical, emotional, and spiritual well-being of immediate as well as extended family members, often in addition to neighbors, friends, church associates, employees and employers, animals, and plants. We do this not merely because we are coerced—though we often are—but because our connections with and the facilitating of life itself is what gives us deepest joy.

Perhaps whatever widespread limiting, debasing, and warping of our generous natures *is* now evident, however, can be traced directly to men's exploitation of this characteristic of female being.

According to Vaughan, gift giving—concentrating on satisfying needs rather than on receiving payment—is for all people "a normal, healthy way to behave," and that, freed from the taint of bribery or blackmail, both giving and receiving can be highly pleasurable.[18] But she is aware that pleasure, though necessary, is not the most

---

[18] Genevieve Vaughan, "The Philosophy Behind Stonehaven (An Attempt to Preach What We Practice)," p. 3.

important result. Gift giving, she maintains, is a real solution to the moral chaos inevitable in patriarchy's exchange mentality. Giving and receiving gifts, we can eliminate the greed, egomania, and fear that are part of the competitive exchange system.[19]

Gifts open the sluice gates of the universe and allow its abundance to stream out. Giving gifts, we can unlock the Nile and let its nutriment-rich flow nourish every part of Earth's ecosystem, physical and spiritual.

Other radical differences between the value systems represented by gift giving and exchange become apparent in the behavior they evoke and the short- and long-term effects of the transactions on individuals and communities. Gift giving creates abundance; exchange produces scarcity. Gift giving protects and nurtures the environment and other species; exchange necessitates their exploitation and destruction. Gift giving encourages ethical, compassionate, and humane individual and group behavior; exchange disconnects and isolates, and encourages expediency. By not assigning value to the gift itself, gift giving discourages greed;[20] by valuing products for their exchange value, exchange promotes avarice and covetousness. Gift giving, by assigning value to the satisfaction of the need and to the connections that are

---

[19] Conversation between Genevieve Vaughan and Susan Horwitz, March 1989.

[20] Genevieve Vaughan, "The Philosophy Behind Stonehaven (An Attempt to Preach What We Practice)," p. 5.

established as the need is met,[21] expands human connections and unity; exchange isolates individuals and encourages an adversarial stance.

A look at bartering as an example of exchange reveals how it discourages community, how its exclusivity creates a closed circuit of interaction and blocks the natural flow of human energy.

Two women exchange objects or services that they agree are of approximately equal value in time or money. Even though it is gentle and barely noticeable, an adversarial attitude is inescapably built into this transaction, coloring the tone of the entire proceeding. When the transaction ends, the experience is over; neither woman ends up with more than she came with, physically or metaphysically. Few spiritual, emotional, intellectual, or ethical ripples go out from it into either their lives or the life of the community. Exchange is like dropping a stone into wet concrete.

On the other hand, since in gift giving no expectation of equivalent return exists to limit or break connections, the gift flows on and out, the circle of givers and receivers expanding exponentially and overlapping in all directions. Every receiver is also a multiple giver, every giver receives many gifts. Giving a gift is like tossing a handful of stones into a calm lake.

In addition to the material plenty that results from gift giving, riches of spirit attend and follow upon it, riches

---

[21] Genevieve Vaughan, "The Philosophy Behind Stonehaven (An Attempt to Preach What We Practice)," p. 6.

that are permanent and available to everyone. In order to give good gifts, for example, people must first notice what others need and care how they feel. Studying what gifts will in fact fill needs or truly give pleasure, they arrive at a common understanding of human needs and how to satisfy them in all their variety, an understanding that links them to all other human beings. This in turn makes their interdependence visible and reveals to them its enormous value.[22]

Equal benefits follow upon the act of receiving. In a gift-giving society, everyone is a receiver from birth as well as a giver. Because both giving and receiving are prized for their indispensable roles in maintaining the free flow of life-sustaining energy, receivers are as conscious as givers of their worthiness. They receive in the sure knowledge that they deserve to have everything they need simply because, like the birds of the air and the lilies of the fields, they are living beings.

In addition to insuring material abundance, therefore, gift giving/receiving yields metaphysical gifts that also flow into the gift stream, blessing everyone in perpetuity: gifts of understanding, compassion, wisdom, and connection. In this way, the female mode—giving as the means of satisfying needs—creates bonds of trust and security on a practical level.[23]

---

[22] Conversation between Genevieve Vaughan and Susan Horwitz, February 1989.

[23] Conversation between Genevieve Vaughan and Susan Horwitz, February 1989.

Gift giving's terrific subversive potential, therefore, lies not only in its ability to satisfy all needs—a condition of abundance that is anathema to patriarchy and would be enough in itself to spell its doom—but also automatically establish connections among people, unite them, and encourage and strengthen community.[24] Because patriarchy depends upon keeping people isolated from and suspicious of one another, it cannot withstand genuine community.

The antithesis of patriarchy is a world of community, and a global community or ecosystem is what women have come to organize.

Vaughan's view that women's nurturing is the basic underlying value system, and one that, though rendered invisible by patriarchy, is alive, venerable, and global reinforces my belief that the model for the world we want is already well-developed among women. What we need to do now is to replace men's constipated "economy" and all its attendant pain and deprivation with our abundance model. Continuing to use Earth's ecosystem as our blueprint, we need to make gift giving the standard method on this globe of converting energy into life.

First, facing the painful reality that for hundreds of years women have not respected femaleness or taken seriously anything associated with women, we must acknowledge the beauty, simplicity, and integrity of our basic way of being. Only then can we acknowledge its

---

[24] Genevieve Vaughan, "The Philosophy Behind Stonehaven (An Attempt to Preach What We Practice)," p. 4.

value and its incredibly transformative potential. Then we must believe in ourselves and our wisdom so fiercely that we begin *now* to practice gift giving on a larger scale than we ever dreamed would be required. Only immersion in it, only daily passionate and courageous experimentation with it by enough of us, can expand women's "economy" into a global reality.

But how do we break out of our transfixed minds, out of what Mary Ann Beall terms "the conservatism of inertia?" [25] We are so embedded in the end game of this particular failure of the fathers called patriarchy that it seems impossible even to frame how we might begin to move out, how we might shift the blockage and start the flow of life again. Nevertheless I believe we must.

I say this in full awareness of the difficulty; I myself cannot see an inch around the corner of this world into the new. But I know that before any blockage disappears from the world, it must first disappear from our minds. Therefore, our initial challenge is to free the possibility of a women's world by making it real to ourselves. In the very act of *perceiving* and *feeling* ourselves as not trapped in men's exchange system, our energy will be unblocked and we can begin to break out. In fact, in some way not amenable to logic this change in our perceptions of what is possible is *in itself* our exodus.

To begin this exodus, we must imagine in broad terms how a nonexchange, gift-giving society might function.

---

[25] Conversation with Mary Ann Beall, March 1989.

239

Trying to conjure such a society in detail will defeat us; we take tainted specifics into any imagined scenario. It is the *spirit* of a women's anarchic world we must imagine, the feeling of it. As visionaries dream, we must dream it sweepingly and unreservedly, anticipating it from our cherished principles and out of the desires of our hearts. Such a combined undertaking of intuition, passion, intelligence, and spirit, by changing our beliefs about what is possible, can free us to turn principle and desire into physical reality.

As a rough start, let us imagine a small town where the foremost desire of the citizenry is that everyone have everything necessary for health and joy. In order to achieve this, everyone in town *does what they want to do all the time,* loyal first to their own welfare while remaining fully aware of their critical interconnection with everyone else's. Under these circumstances chances are very good that, like a gigantic feminist potluck dinner, there will be enough of everything and all needs will be met with minimum time or effort spent by any one individual. It is only a matter of maintaining the flow. Functioning within the design of the natural world is always the simplest and most effective plan.

Nature's gift-giving design requires neither printing of money nor elaborate schemes for figuring out equivalent values. It necessitates no bureaucracy at all. What is does require is a deep love for life and all living things, for their individual and interconnected, interdependent rhythms, cycles, and energies. It requires a profound respect for oneself and faith that the springs of one's inner power loop through and among those of every other part of the universe, from the Milky Way's innumerable systems to the newborn kittens under the porch. It requires the fearless delight in ambiguity that comes from immersion in the present and that renders regulation and its requisite hierarchy not only irrelevant but odious.

Let us look at a young woman in this town who has recently arrived from a house of contemplation in the countryside without a definite idea of what she might enjoy doing now. She looks the community's situation over, perhaps consulting with others, to see what talents are in short supply and what the community needs. Finding a need that pleases her to turn her abilities to, she prepares to fill the gap.

Let us say that in this case the town needs another shoemaker and that she becomes one, but only for as long as it gives her satisfaction. In this town, no one is expected to repeat the same creative act their entire adult lives unless they wish to.

Now that she is a shoemaker, she offers to make shoes. When anyone in the town needs shoes, they can now go to her workshop. She measures their feet, listens to their description of the style, color, material they prefer, and then makes shoes for them. They do not give her anything in return when they take those shoes home with them. But each of them also has some function (or functions) in the community from which she will benefit in turn, though perhaps not directly. Like them, whenever she needs something, all she needs to do is get it from the appropriate person or place.

In this town, I'm a dentist. Because my daughter makes wonderful shoes for me, I have no need to request shoes from any of the shoemakers in town. But when the new shoemaker needs her teeth repositioned, she nevertheless comes to me and I make braces for her. The wire for the braces is drawn by a local metal worker with perfect teeth (who will therefore probably never need my services) who, among other things, supplies toolheads to the woman in the community who crafts their wooden handles and makes them available to the rest of us.

Because everyone in town does what they enjoy all the time, when you, who are a poet, are having a professional hair cut, you have the satisfaction of knowing that the woman cutting your hair isn't forced into doing it by the necessity of feeding her kids. You can be sure that she chooses to cut every hair she cuts because she likes and wants to. You can assume that she is there also because she enjoys sharing her gifts with others, because she understands her connection with them, aware that by contributing to their well-being she contributes to her own, and because she gets satisfaction from being an integral part of the life of the community.

Knowing the philosophy of the town you therefore know that if she didn't want to be cutting your hair, she wouldn't be. She would be doing something else. Or perhaps she would be doing nothing at all while she thought over what she would like to do, or while she merely contemplated the miracle of her existence.

No one in town keeps track of anyone else's activities—what they contribute to and take from community resources. It is assumed that everyone is a responsible person and perfectly able to regulate themselves. No one questions whether others are "working" enough or doing "their share" because no one presumes to understand better than the person in question what is meant by "working" and what "their share" might be. In fact, the word "work" cannot be found in the town's vocabulary. People simply do what they enjoy doing and in the natural flow of things their every need is met.

In a society where everyone monitors themselves, no one presumes to know what anyone needs more than that person herself. Everyone's decisions are respected and honored. No one needs to give or to get permission. This society works because everyone respects everyone else, everyone cares about everyone else, everyone desires everyone else's happiness and health as much as they desire their own, and everyone understands the interconnectedness of their well-being with that of others and of all living things.

Artists make art, music, literature, drama for their own and the community's pleasure, and even many of those whose major focus is something else take their artistic talents seriously and use them for their own and others' delight. Philosophers think; they may also write and talk to one another and to anyone who comes by for that purpose. And many *do* come by because people here know that each of them is not only capable of important thinking but also of finding excitement and satisfaction in rigorous thought. Contemplatives meditate, and everybody else knows that they too can take however much time they want simply to drift and dream. No one automatically assumes that if someone sits quietly under a tree day after day for months or even years merely gazing out upon the scene that she is not "doing" anything useful or enriching for the community. Everyone knows that such times—and sometimes many such times of gathering one's life around oneself in silence—are crucial for every living thing and therefore for the ecology of all systems, including their own community. They know that whole lifetimes of such quiet inwardness are needed by some people.

People in this town, in fact, have found that they enjoy life more and are more likely to flourish when they model their cycles of energy upon the cycles of the natural world. During the winter, therefore, everyone slows down, sleeps more and eats less, spends more time in quiet reflection—retreats into a sort of physical and spiritual hibernation. When this gestation time gives way to germination in the spring, creative projects of all sorts burst forth. These blossom throughout the summer. Then in the fall, a great winding up of affairs takes place, a cleaning off of the slate so that winter's rest may be uncluttered, peaceful, and replenishing.

Because the value that above all others informs behavior in this town is that everyone have what they need for health and joy, and because there is no hierarchy to block the flow that provides this, there is no incentive to consume more than one needs. Neither is there any motivation to create artificial needs in others by inflating their desires; no propaganda, that is, dedicated to confusing and separating wants and needs—tricking people into believing that they *need* things when they really only *want* them to satisfy some externally engineered craving for superiority and control.

When needs are real, not manufactured and manipulated to provide a surplus for someone else, wants and needs are identical. In this town, therefore, people know what they truly need. Nobody hoards 40 pairs of shoes in their closet, for instance. They want shoes for the purpose shoes are needed—to beautify and protect their feet. The paradox is that when ownership is inconsequential, everyone feels as if they own enough.

In addition, since "things" are no longer believed to have the ability to fill up emotional emptiness—no ads persuade subliminally that certain perfumes or clothes or copiers guarantee intimacy or success—acquisitiveness is not mistaken for a shortcut to healing sickness of the soul.

For this and other reasons, the things the townspeople *do* own give them a great deal of satisfaction. They probably know personally most of the artisans and crafters, the artists and musicians who make what they use. Perhaps when they are considering owning something, they watch or assist its maker, always thereafter connecting her wares with her, her unique personality and gifts, and the personal connection they made with her. This closeness—in world view as well as in geography— to the actual makers and to the process of creation gives them an appreciation of the abilities that are required, causes them to honor the maker, her talent and labor, and to rejoice in the use of her creation. Their enjoyment of owning is in this way based upon entirely different criteria from those applied in exchange cultures.

In this society, because everyone's resources and talents are free to everyone else, not only do the gifts create a luxurious abundance for everyone of everything, but the members of the community also give one another the most precious gift of them all, an abundance of time. When they broke the tyranny of money in this town, they also ended the tyranny of Father time. They are now in control of their own lives and therefore they are in control of their own time. They feel no frenzy and are never "beside themselves." Instead they are always "inside themselves"—centered, alive, and experiencing themselves and others entirely in the present.

Controlling time, they do not allow time to force them on a mad march from this side of the day to that and off into the night where it reluctantly drops them, raw and unfinished, on their beds in the dark. They do not obey the clock here or live by its dictates. No one wears a wristwatch. They make no appointments. Healers, hairdressers, tailors, dentists—all who supply services to the community—are available during certain parts of certain days. When townspeople drop by then and find someone waiting before them, they stop and chat or sit and rest in the sunshine or read awhile in the library or plant some bulbs along the path or write a poem until their turn.

They know that having not just enough but an abundance of time is the cornerstone of their freedom.

I began this chapter with thoughts about time, Father time in particular, and how patriarchy manipulates time (which is both life and money) to create the scarcity necessary for oppression. But I have other, happier, more hopeful thoughts about time and its relation to plenty and peace.

I believe that for hundreds of thousands of years before patriarchy, time was "Mother time," perceived by humans as rich, abundant, and shimmeringly alive, loosely spiral, deeply and freely associative, sensorially satisfying, connective and restful—like dancing effortlessly in warm space among stars.

I long for a world governed again by womb time, warm time, free time, life time, gift time, Mother time. I long for a regulation-free world of self-governing people. I long for anarchy, and I believe there is only one way to have it.

It seems to me, as it has seemed to women before me, that only by combining our dreams, our energy, and our material and cultural resources in self-designed and self-created communities with one another can we hope to free enough time for enough women to restructure the hologram and make tyranny an anachronism.

That we will do this, that we will begin now, and that because this is our appointed hour we will succeed beyond our wildest expectations—this is the dream that sustains me.

CHAPTER 21

Dancing in Our Paradigm Shifts

F or several years now when women have asked me
the inevitable "But what shall we *do*?" the vision
that has flown into my mind is of women coming together
in small groups all over the world, pooling our resources,
building communities of many different sorts and living
together in them in a consciously feminist (i.e., woman-
like) way. I see these womanhelixes strewn starlike
across the Milky Way of the world's cities, towns, and
countrysides, each autonomous in its particular purpose
and design but connected to all the others—perhaps by
technology, but certainly by frequent visits and living
exchanges, by lively interaction, and most important, by
intuitive genius.

Believing that one day soon they will exist, I think of
what such a world community of women will mean to our
individual lives, what freedom it will bring each of us.

Straddling the gulf between two worlds and for awhile yet still having a foot in patriarchy, to begin the work of bringing them into being we will at first need a surplus of material goods and property. Those of us who have dowers in patriarchy will therefore have to transfer them from the old-world side of the gulf to the new.

When we pool our resources—when we can bring ourselves to break from that last patriarchal hook of materialism in some way that honors each of our origins, all our pasts—we will immediately produce abundance for every woman who chooses to join us.

But, you say, only women who have little material wealth will find such a plan inviting. I know that that cynicism reflects a certain reality, but I also know that more and more women, seeing that Earth will soon be sick beyond recovery or destroyed outright in unthinkably hideous ways, are ready now to dare anything. For instance, as we die of cancer like flies, what, we ask ourselves, have we to *lose*? Why do we hold on to material things when risking them could mean life, and *good* life, for everyone? Where is the greater risk?

It seems to me that there is nothing left for the free women of the world to do except come together in every community to build—literally and directly—a natural habitat for women. We already know that because women's isolation and alienation from other women are integral parts of our old world programming, each woman's doing her own thing alone, no matter how noble, cannot bring about a new world. Therefore, wanting the new mind to be characterized by connectedness, wholeness, and trust, by cooperation and interdependence, we will choose values and methods that are also characterized by genuine community. Because how we do it is what we will get, women's world calls for women *together*, side by side, planning, growing, changing, building.

How and when will such communities come into being? Who will build them and where? What will they look like? How will they function?

There are, of course, still some feminists who will not—perhaps cannot—even *consider* these questions. As far as they are concerned, this is in the realm of science fiction. But these are the very questions feminism demands that we ask ourselves, and many of us are searching for the answers.

We search because we know that a loving, peaceful world is possible, and not only in science fiction. We know this because we have learned to be peaceful and loving ourselves. In doing this, we have created a new world inside us and around us where we live. In each of our own hearts, freedom is becoming more fully realized every moment, so that surrounding us now—in our energy fields, everywhere our auras touch—are the beginnings of some distinct, new, and beneficent reality. We know that immense and rapid restructuring of reality is possible because we have radically restructured the world of our own lives.

When women ask me "What shall we do?" I don't think they are really asking me to tell them what to do; they know I can only answer "Live today as you want the world to be." None of us knows for certain how we will act when we are free; the only thing we can be sure of is that none of us will be doing the same things we did before, and that there will be much variety: we won't *all* be doing even the same *new* things.

Like the rest of us, the women who ask that question know that absolutely nothing is working for women "out there," that all the passion and effort, all the promises, all the hopes have essentially come to nothing for women as a global caste. Even the minute reforms we thought we could make have turned out to be pipe dreams. And as patriarchy reigns undaunted, the words "feminism" and "feminist" are scarcely heard any more in the land. When they *are* heard, they refer to women who are *passing* in men's world. All our protesting, our challenging, our demanding, our playing the game—all our collaborative resistance—has succeeded only in bringing us to 1989 with fierce misogynists in the White House, SDI funded by Congress, and men's tolerance of abortion well on its way out of existence.

Change requires a margin of safety, and that margin has narrowed appreciably in the last decade. The fear of reprisals, the fear of men's presumed "power," now rages in the land, and because fear begets pessimism, despair is numbing many hearts. Women who were once activists are guiltily justifying inaction or playing the game by thinking, "There is nothing I can do about this. I may as well grab what little happiness I can for myself" as they retreat into their jobs, their children, their romantic attachments.

But death of desire is death of the heart, and women

after all cannot relinquish their longing for a womanly world any more than they can make their indomitable hearts stop beating. So though they can see no basic change in society, and though in fact women's condition seems to be steadily deteriorating, women question me hoping to find reason to believe again. Women who are changing in more radical ways every day long for evidence to support my assertion that by changing ourselves we really *can* change the world.

But if my assertion—that as we change ourselves we change reality—and the theory of dissipative structures[1] are both correct, the evidence we long for may not be available; the profound revision of the external world we desire is probably not going to be observable day by day in small increments. Instead, when enough of us make the necessary shifts in our individual thought, perception, and feeling, then the ideas, perceptions, and feelings of the whole society will shift rapidly, almost all at once, in the direction we have been pioneering.

The analogy of the hatching of a baby chick is also helpful in clarifying this phenomenon. As it grows from embryo to fetus inside the egg, on the outside nothing whatever appears to be changing. Even when the chick begins to peck its way through the shell, it is not until its

---

[1] The most credible theory of social change I know, this posits that oppressive systems function by dissipating the energies and loyalties of the various groups of people that compose them. Because of this, they cannot survive integration, connection, or unity among and between these groups. (Marilyn Ferguson, Ed. "Brain/Mind Bulletin," Vol. 4, No. 13, May 21, 1979, p. 1.)

beak actually breaks the surface that change is evident. By that time the chick is fully formed and embarking on a life of its own—an apparently instantaneous development.

Perhaps this is the reason that, though many women are living already in a new mind and with their lives creating a new dimension of human experience, involved in the most rapid and prodigious internal revolution ever seen on this planet, little of it is yet observable as change at the root of society. We all wish to believe, of course, that though we cannot see it deep change is actually occurring beneath the shell.

In Albuquerque at Wiminfest in 1988 when Alix talked to Susan and me about meeting the aboriginal Australian women she was especially excited about their rituals.

Believing that at the beginning of time and for hundreds of thousands of years thereafter all Earth's people were women, in their sacred rituals these women now invoke that time and their ancient counterparts.

By holding it firmly in memory, they keep their history dynamic and continuous, they know their place in the scheme of things, they retain the vision of themselves as characters in a human saga of what to us would be unthinkable antiquity.

Imagine women whose sense of self has not been nearly obliterated by men's violence! Such women have existed for millennia before us, still exist in small pockets such as this. Imagine how we would be, what we would do, if we were such women now.

The paradox is that even as we reel from men's brutality, we *are* such women.

My dream is that women will create the world again, that we will be "original" women,[2] originating now what we need for ourselves. Part of doing that is, as those aboriginal women teach us, to invoke the women of our own past, from the beginning to our time—the Beguines and nuns we know about,[3] as well as the priestesses and others who preceded them and about whom we can only surmise—who chose to be part of a women's experiment in conscious creation of world. I remember them with gratitude. I honor them here.

I want also to remember their spiritual descendants, the feminist pioneers who in our own time have formed both rural and urban communities of one kind or another to investigate, protect, and serve the interests of women. I am simultaneously awestruck and exhilarated by the daring of their extraordinary vision and by the willingness with which they followed it to the farthest, most isolated fringes of the Women's Movement.

I am humbled by their loyalty to an internal mandate that kept them radically out of step with conventional feminism and estranged them from those of their sisters embroiled in inevitably fruitless campaigns for women's civil rights. I honor these women for their early under-

---

[2] Janice Raymond, *A Passion for Friends: Toward a Philosophy of Female Affection*. Beacon Press: Boston, 1986, p. 35.

[3] Janice Raymond, *A Passion for Friends: Toward a Philosophy of Female Affection*, chapter 2.

255

standing that the very nature of patriarchy prevents us from redesigning or reforming it to include women or our ways, for their consequent wise refusal to be drawn by resistance into the vampire system's dangerous dance, and for their bravery in trusting themselves and other women to figure out and to learn to live in a more balanced spiritual and economic ecology.

Though few of the many feminist communities born in such hope in the late 60s and early 70s survive,[4] interest in women's communities is on the rise again. More and more of us are realizing that nothing we were told to expect, none of the great reformations feminism was going to make in society and in women's lives, has come to pass or indeed *can* come to pass in the patriarchal system. Every woman who wakes to the knowledge that we have not yet moved patriarchy so much as one hair off its destructive timetable is that much closer to joining with her sisters and taking the world into her own hands.

As many of us think again about coming together to build a society based on women's values, we need to look as closely as we can at the reasons that so many of those first attempts failed. When we do, I think we will discover that, not surprisingly, most smashed upon the overlapping reefs of internalized oppression and economic dependence.

Over the years I have been told tales of the demise of those early communities. As I listened, the outlines of the

---

[4] Some, of course, are still alive, and their members as committed as ever to living in ways they perceive as authentic for women.

tragedy gradually appeared, revealing how thoroughly our programming to hate women warps our ability to recognize that what women do *matters* and that it matters *incalculably*, and how consistently and hugely our internalizing of society's beliefs about femaleness causes us to underrate our own and other women's ideas and efforts.

Some experiments, women tell me, failed simply because not enough women were interested in participating. Tensions over money, differences in class perspectives, and ownership hierarchy escalated unbearably in others. Racism and classism were endemic, and their converse, victim hierarchy, was not uncommon (i.e., the idea that whoever had been the most brutalized by patriarchy deserved most respect, power, and material advantage in the group). Women were often unwilling to suspend personal biases so that the group purpose could be served. They had difficulty disagreeing without assigning blame and moral turpitude. Too often they could not figure out how to differ and still be part of a cohesive group. Communication was hampered by differences among women in their willingness not only to take responsibility but even to agree about the *necessity* of taking responsibility for themselves or for devising and carrying out community rules. In short, they were characterized by wide variation in conscious or unconscious definitions of anarchy and in personal readiness for living it.

I have been assailed with accounts of endless wrangles over the meaning of feminism and the interpretation and application of feminist theory to everyday life, wrangles that often seemed to turn into Ms. Most Politically

Correct competitions.

These and dozens of other thorns repeatedly punctured the dream. When the pain grew too fierce, we did what we have been trained to do: we abandoned our game.

In *A Different Voice,* Carol Gilligan cites Janet Lever's observations of girls on the playground and her documentation of what I call girls' "quit the game syndrome." Lever found that disagreements over rules do not succeed in making boys quit the game. On the contrary, boys learn to enjoy the legal wrangle about rules as much as they enjoy playing. When disagreements arise in girls' games, however, they disband. Lever's analysis is that because girls have different values, valuing relationships more than they value rules and games, they refuse to risk alienating others by going through the charged process necessary to settle disputes.[5]

I think there is another way to view these data. We know that patriarchy undermines relationships between females by consistently programming us to despise and compete with other women and girls and instead to bestow our trust and respect upon men and their games.[6] I believe the basic difference between boys and girls that

[5] Carol Gilligan, *In a Different Voice.* Harvard University Press: Cambridge, MA, 1982, p. 10.

[6] Though lesbians sometimes think we are excluded from this unconscious behavior by virtue of our sexual interest in women and disinterest in men, we are often as disparaging of women and as impressed with and imitative of what we perceive as male power as any women. Being Lesbians does not inure us against what Janice Raymond terms hetero-relational attitudes and behavior (*A Passion for Friends: Toward a Philosophy of Female Affection,* p. 11).

accounts for what researchers observed on playgrounds is that, unlike boys, girls do not take themselves or their activities seriously at all.

Because they consider their games significant, boys are willing to risk conflict and endure angry confrontations so that their game can go on. Girls, on the other hand, view their games as not only insignificant but as "not-real" games anyway—male norms and competitive models being always the criteria. Because of this, in the face of difficulties girls simply quit. They have internalized the major message of patriarchy that female stuff is not important enough to take risks for.

This is internalized oppression and is, I believe, the culprit in the failure of female communities to take hold with genuine resilience and vigor. I think it explains why there are not yet tens of thousands of strong women's communities in this country.

In most of the first women's communities that sprang up at the beginning of the second wave of feminism in this century, we were not able to establish a new world order because we unwittingly took this old-world mind with us, we carried our slave habits with us into the wilderness. Simply changing locations couldn't and didn't heal the heart that had become self-loathing from incest and other family torture, from addictions, from poverty, from rape, and from the staggering effects of female acculturation in the public school system and in phallus-stroking churches. Being with others like ourselves only made easier the projection of our self-hatred, our internalized oppression, upon them.

Many women came out of their community experiment grim with disillusionment. It had been far more complex and painful than they had anticipated. Though consciousness-raising groups were in their heyday, and though many feminists were madly theorizing and up to their ears in "actions," few of us were aware of how completely *we* were going to have to change. It took us nearly two decades to understand how deep and truly transformative our revolution had to be in our personal lives before it could manifest itself as some new order in the external world.

In those early days we were full of passion and energy and dedication, but we were also driven by rage, pain, and fear, by confusion and anchorlessness. We projected these states upon one another then under the guise of "issues" just as we do now. We do well what the oppressed are trained so well to do—oppress.

Although we like to think that oppressed people, out of their longing for freedom, come to understand freedom better than those who have always been free, the truth is that we learn what we live. Women have lived oppression. What we know best, therefore, is how to oppress—how to keep ourselves and other women from freedom. No one learns liberty from bondage, only the burning lust for it. Lusting for freedom does not teach us the dynamics of being free or of allowing freedom to others. Eating, drinking, and sleeping oppression as individuals since birth and as a caste for millennia, the women who bravely set out to create free and loving communities for women had been transmogrified in a thousand subtle ways by their captors into collaborators in their own and one another's torture.

So it is hardly any wonder that women were no more successful than they were in those days in establishing a literal new women's world. Having no conscious new plans to follow, they were led all unaware by patriarchy's oldest and deepest program: hate yourself. Hate women. Hurt, distrust, and thwart all that is female.

In addition, the entire movement then had too little understanding of the dynamics of women's oppression, viewing men and their violent degradation of us as the sole factor in our low status. For the first decade, this perspective kept the Women's Movement victim oriented and reactive, dictated almost entirely by male behavior— for instance, if they voted against us, we shook our fists on camera, marched, and protested.

It took nearly a decade for most of us to realize that we had internalized men's violence and debasement of us in such a way that we carried out antiwoman dicta against ourselves and our sisters *on our own*. We saw to our horror that we didn't need men's atrocities against us any longer in order to feel victimized; we were victims[7] in our feelings and perceptions about ourselves, in our attitudes

---

[7] It could be argued here that some women really *are* victims. I would counter that, rather, they are victim*ized*, oppressed. Perceiving oneself or anyone else as a victim is a *choice*, a decision to take a particular ontological stance. Unfortunately, this is the stance women are taught to take about females in sadistic society. This is why the largest part of our reprogramming has to do with perceiving ourselves not as acted upon but as powerful actors and doers.

and behavior. We realized that by viewing the world and all our experience through victim-eyes, we behaved in ways that perpetuated our powerlessness and exploitation.

So though the idea of community may have been perfect, the timing of the first flurry of experiments was not. Our movement was too young. Women needed time to move from our initial defensive, dependent, internally oppressed stance to readiness for responsibility—responsibility to overcome our deep training to tear one another to pieces and to unite. We needed time to begin taking responsibility not to try to get men to change the world but to rebuild it ourselves as we wished it to be. We needed time to stop seeing ourselves as victims powerless against an overwhelming male structure. We needed time to stop thinking small, expecting too little of ourselves, dreaming and daring on a drastically reduced scale, as slavery had taught us to do. We needed time to reach a point in our internal revolution where we were willing—even eager—to let go of those self-fulfilling and self-defeating expectations and opinions and to replace them with awareness of our own tremendous power to do together whatever we chose to do.

Freedom means having more than one option. The Women's Movement is above all else about freedom, about increasing the number of women's choices. A choice is to build our own complete society on totally different bases, a literal new world. I can think of no more effective method of ridding ourselves of our internalized oppression. To do it we will have to take ourselves and other women seriously. We will have to see women as major actors on the world's stage.

More than that, we will have to live in an awareness of our cosmic importance, learning to govern ourselves with freedom—as is women's way—rather than with the compulsion that is men's.

I want to join with women to make a world that reflects us from ground to sky and then to invite all women into that free world. I want to invite women to come home at last.

I am not alone in this desire. Today again hundreds of our prophetic pioneers are making determined, courageous attempts to create a wholesome society, to live together in new ways, designing and testing models of cooperative, loving self-government. I am grateful to them for believing in themselves and in us, for the daily courage it takes to pry open the old universe and wrest forth new choices for women. I thank them for practicing how to live wild and free, so that wildness and freedom are more possible for the rest of us. I congratulate them for not quitting the game.

But more than that, I think they are right, that the fastest, surest, and most effective way to bring about the new world, the world in which women are free in our souls as well as in our society, is for us to come together and create that world, basing it on women's values, mode of being, and world view, building communities to provide for women what we want and need: abundance, peerness, independence, power to affect the external world as well as to direct our own lives, room for experiments in living in various ways with other women, and time and space to contemplate and savor our experience.

Because they are so absolutely crucial to a fulfillment of feminism's purpose on our planet at this time, I look at the women's communities that I know of—the failed, the still functioning but struggling, those trying to acquire land to begin in earnest, those newly born and still starry-eyed—and I am surprised at their isolation in the Women's Movement. I am surprised that they seem not to be part of the general feminist agenda, that this agenda does not include *centrally* the creation of an entirely new and comprehensive model of human interaction. I can hardly believe that so many strong and wonderful women are still trying to make room for women in men's game—revealing their lack of self-knowledge and self-esteem and their feelings of powerlessness—when there is a marvelous women's game going on out there.

I watch small groups of women struggling to pay for pieces of land, trying to get the rest of us to understand the importance of having a place to practice feminism uninterruptedly together. That is, a place to practice being free of patriarchal dicta in everything they do and say, to practice creating a harmonious, nonhierarchical, gift-giving women's world by living in it moment to moment.

Watching, I see women who might facilitate this new reality giving their money and time instead to the male game—men's politics and revolutions, the old woman-hating, hierarchical, competitive world. I watch with pain as they pour their resources back into patriarchy out of a deep and largely denied belief in the inferiority of women and the power of men.

Perhaps some of the general lack of enthusiasm about women's communities among many feminists is that these communities are perceived as Lesbian or separatist and therefore not relevant to heterosexual, bisexual, or non-separatist women. Also, because many of these communities are "on the land," perhaps other reasons for apathy are that many women do not find the idea of agrarian life appealing, understand how they can have what they need to live, or believe they can find intellectual or social stimulation with a small group in relative seclusion.

It is true that an overwhelming majority of women who choose to experiment with living outside patriarchy are Lesbians; trying to live with men outside patriarchy seems almost a contradiction in terms—anywhere men are, to one degree or another so is the expectation and assumption of male privilege that is patriarchy.[8]

In the meantime, it makes good sense for women who do not have to fear losing their loved men or their "docile prisoner" privileges, to take the most risks. It is also in line with a noble tradition in the Women's Movement as well as in the world in general for Lesbians to explore the wilderness, to clear, prepare, and smooth the way for others. Feminists of all political and sexual persuasions understand that the Women's Movement would not exist at all if no women had dared to center the whole of their

---

[8] But women and well-intentioned men *are* experimenting together, and perhaps in time I will be able to see more clearly the value of that effort.

lives around women.

Many Lesbians who pick up their backpacks and hike off to "women's land" somewhere must be motivated at least in part by the desire to find a place where women are valued for themselves, not for the men or male garrisons they are servicing, a place where hetero-relations are not enforced by violence and terrorism. There are undoubtedly other incentives: to be close to nature, to be in a society from dawn to dawn that is consciously trying to live differently, and to learn together how to put feminist theory into practice. Most of them surely want to be as independent as possible of men's economy, knowing that self-reliance brings confidence and self-knowledge. Many want to "discover [their] discontent" and to break out of "oppressive roles and images,"[9] simplifying their lives and living them on the basis of nonmaterialistic values.

That to do this they indeed have to "separate" themselves from that society might qualify them all as separatists. Some openly and proudly take that name upon themselves, knowing that it is essential for the continuing development of our purpose that some of us escape as completely as we can, physically and economically as well as intellectually and emotionally, from men and their iniquitous mind. Others of us who have stayed behind and have forsaken hetero-relations in as many areas of our lives as possible, may or may not think of

---

[9] "Country Women," Vol 1, No. 1, Albion, CA, October 1972.

ourselves as separatists.

I haven't asked why others do not, so I can only give my reasons for not adopting the separatist label myself. Daily—even hourly—I am discarding my patriarchal baggage, leaving it piece by piece behind me as thoroughly as if I'd tossed it into another dimension. Part of this rejected baggage is defining myself in relation to men. Because "separatist" defines me in relation to men and their system—separate from *them*, separate from *that*—I do not call myself a separatist.

But what I do or do not call myself is irrelevant now when women of all varieties, colors, abilities, ages, and classes, whether Lesbian or separatist or not, must come together in harmonious diversity to "restore and rebalance women's ecology of values." [10]

Given, however, that all the "issues" from self-hatred to racism to internalized powerlessness plague our movement now just as they did at the beginning, can we realistically expect to establish communities and ultimately another society any more successfully today than most of the women who tried and failed yesterday? Is there any reason to believe that we can work together any better now?

I think so. For one thing, we have the lessons learned by the women who tried before us—no small inheritance for would-be goddesses. We have learned a great deal about ourselves and about our condition in the last

---

[10] Hazel Henderson, *The Politics of the Solar Age: Alternatives to Economics,* p. 16.

decade: we have faced our own sexism, owned up to our racism, healed from incest, cast off our addictions, discovered our spiritual powers, erased from our behavior the patterns we developed to help us cope in flawed families, and trusted ourselves as we trust the other forces in the universe.

We have listened to one another more attentively and with greater care, realizing how much depended upon it. We have acknowledged and tried to understand our differences and to perceive diversity as positive, learning in the process to love one another across the many barriers patriarchy erects between us.

Each of us has, in short, been deeply involved in her own internal, personal revolution and through it has grown strong and unafraid. Many of us have grown daily more aware of how central the success of our internal work is to the success of our external purposes and that we will therefore have to continue it with varying intensity until the day we die.

Doing our internal work has already taught us the most important lesson, that the capacity of each of us to be healthily and happily alone precedes being successfully together in community, just as loving oneself precedes loving others.

It is because of our knowledge now that the world must first change inside us that our experiments in creating a woman's world have so much better chance of succeeding this time around.

Even if it were a slim chance—and I think it is not slim but *enormous*—it is one we must take. We have no alternative and never really have had. From the onset of patriarchy's siege against us, women's choice has been either to create a safe, nourishing environment for ourselves or to die. For the most part up to now we have chosen to die—on all the levels that women die.

Now it is time to stop dying, time to do something different, time to live. Experimenting with how to live fully, freely, abundantly, and in harmony with one another as women and with all other living things is certainly something different. In fact, it is something so fresh and exciting and so right up our alley, a challenge so fitting to our talents and necessity, that I wonder as I write why any of us would choose to do anything else. Why would any woman choose to continue to live isolated in the daily boredom and ugliness of men's dull and violent world rather than to take hands with her sisters in the most fascinating, intensely satisfying, boldest, and most ennobling possible activity?

On occasion when I have said this, some woman counters: "That's all very well to say, but how do you suggest we do it? Patriarchy is too strong, too pervasive."

I remind her that patriarchy, or god culture, is only about 5,000 years old. But whatever the date of its birth, in historical terms it is a mere mewling infant.

Women's culture, on the other hand, based on the life-enhancing values of the Great Mother, the goddess who was once worshipped by everyone on planet Earth, is incalculably ancient and deeply embedded in the memory of our species. It is probably the most powerful and widespread social organization and world view in human experience, prevailing and flourishing as it did across the entire globe for at least 200,000 years before men began their war games.

Then, in the midst of this mighty civilization, men created patriarchy, the dance of death, the antithesis of the choreography of women's mind as it had been universally actualized.

If *men* could create a different world under such daunting circumstances, clearly *women* can expect nothing but wildest success in building our own in the midst of patriarchy, the all-time cultural runt.

Our task will be made easier because the essence of women's archaic world is still here. Where would it have gone in this space/time ellipse that has no boundaries, no beginning and no end, this universe where there is no way to get off or out because there is no such thing as "out," no such place as "off"? If that mind, that way of being, is still here, as it must be, it must also be possible for us to refine and purify our consciousness enough to step into it.

Women say fearfully, "But men own all the resources! We've got to get them from them in order to live." But there is only one condition on which this is entirely true, and that is if we stay in their system. So long as we remain slaves, men *do* own all the resources. When we escape, we take ourselves—their primary resources—with us for our own enrichment.

Many, many of us are now focused on our escape. Having divested ourselves of our fear of patriarchy, having rid ourselves of our obsession with it, having ferreted out its agents in our personal lives and shown them the door, centering calmly in our own power, we are ready, *more* than ready, *long past* ready, to try a new experiment in living together in freedom.

We realize more and more often, as we move ever farther from the psychic center of patriarchy, that direction comes only if we take the first brave steps in faith. Empty-handed, open-minded, unhampered by expectations—this is the only state that allows us the flexibility to change and grow moment by moment into people of a mind that is in the best possible sense alien to the prevailing mind. Our daring to proceed into the wilderness mapless, guided only by our internal voices, is what will change us into people who are not afraid of the unfamiliar, people who do not need to be led and governed, people who can recognize and heed the guidance of their own uncorruptible spirits.

The answers our spirits give us are always about our own personal power. They teach us that we can't finish this job of coming into the knowledge and control of our full power until we actually watch ourselves create a world. There is no way for us to find answers except by taking our turn at world-making now that the men have—thank goodness—finished theirs.

To believe we are goddesses, we are going to have to do some goddess work. Now in the coda of men's dead march, we are going to have to take off our shrouds, slip into our beautiful new paradigm shifts, and dance the dance of life.

I dream that all over the world women are getting

271

their dance ensembles together: finding the other risk-takers, the other fearless, self-loving women in their communities, and examining the possibilities for living economically and emotionally independent of patriarchy. I dream that they are developing processes of interacting that will weld them into a sisterhood so firm that nothing can separate them. I dream of the worlds they spin, the universe they weave, out of the strands of their splendid women's minds and spirits.

As I dream, I whisper a promise to myself: "I will live to see women's spirit sweep over the earth like wildfire: out of men's control, untamable, cleansing, renewing, awakening. I will live to see women walking hand in hand the world over. I will live to see us *free!*"

With this book I end a passage of my life and begin another. As I prepare to turn off the computer and clear the papers away, I know that all the women on Earth are also engaged in winding up the passage of women's collective life under patriarchy and are giving birth to another.

As we draw men's era to a close and open up our own, let us call upon the Mothers, the women who preceded us and those who will follow, to hold us safe now as we love one another in the midst of unspeakable peril.

And let us command the fierce powers of earth and ocean, sky and fire to be with each brave band of us as we become one more flame in the wildfire of femaleness that is blazing through the universe, reshaping the proud and passionate order of things and reforging the human soul.

INDEX

277

About the Author

Although she received her doctorate from Rutgers in 1965, Sonia Johnson is prouder of her 1979 graduation summa cum laude from the Mormon church, the world's foremost university for patriarchal studies.

Catapulted overnight into national prominence, she became a radical feminist, agitating, writing, and establishing a reputation for being one of the great orators of our time. Since her excommunication, she has been speaking professionally at colleges and universities and for a wide variety of organizations and groups.

Her first book, *From Housewife to Heretic*, the story of the excommunication, was published by Doubleday in 1980 and has now been reissued by Wildfire Books. Her second, *Going Out of Our Minds: The Metaphysics of Liberation*, a revolutionary theory of change, was published in 1987 by The Crossing Press.

Inquiries about speaking engagements, workshops, and tapes of speeches should be directed to Susan Horwitz, P.O. Box 10286, Albuquerque, New Mexico 87184, (505) 344-4790.

SONIA JOHNSON BOOKS

———————————— Book Titles ————————————

☐ *From Housewife to Heretic*, 416 pages $10.95

☐ *Going Out of Our Minds: The Metaphysics
of Liberation*, 359 pages $10.95

☐ "Telling the Truth," (pamphlet) 24 pages .... $ 3.00

☐ *Wildfire: Igniting the She/Volution*, 294 pages $10.95

SONIA JOHNSON SPEECHES ON TAPE

———————————— Audio Cassettes ————————————

☐ Sonia Speaks: From Housewife to Heretic, 80 minutes .. $ 9.95

☐ Sonia Speaks: Telling the Truth, 60 minutes .... $ 9.95

☐ Sonia Speaks: Going *Farther* Out of Our Minds,
90 minutes .... $ 9.95

———————————— Video Cassette ————————————

☐ Sonia Speaks: Going *Farther* Out of Our Minds,
100 minutes $29.95

ORDERING INSTRUCTIONS

Check off boxes to indicate selection. Order Amount: _____

Shipping and Handling: Books $1.75: _____

Audio Tapes $1.50: _____

Video Tape $1.75: _____

Amount Enclosed: _____

Please forward your order to: Sonia Johnson, P.O. Box 10286A,
Albuquerque, NM 87184, (505) 344-4790

SONIA JOHNSON BOOKS

————————————— Book Titles —————————————

☐ *From Housewife to Heretic*, 416 pages $10.95

☐ *Going Out of Our Minds: The Metaphysics
   of Liberation*, 359 pages $10.95

☐ "Telling the Truth," (pamphlet) 24 pages .... $ 3.00

☐ *Wildfire: Igniting the She/Volution*, 294 pages $10.95

SONIA JOHNSON SPEECHES ON TAPE

————————————— Audio Cassettes —————————————

☐ Sonia Speaks: From Housewife to Heretic, 80 minutes .. $ 9.95

☐ Sonia Speaks: Telling the Truth, 60 minutes .... $ 9.95

☐ Sonia Speaks: Going *Farther* Out of Our Minds,
   90 minutes .... $ 9.95

————————————— Video Cassette —————————————

☐ Sonia Speaks: Going *Farther* Out of Our Minds,
   100 minutes $29.95

ORDERING INSTRUCTIONS

Check off boxes to indicate selection. Order Amount: _____

Shipping and Handling: Books $1.75: _____

Audio Tapes $1.50: _____

Video Tape $1.75: _____

Amount Enclosed: _____

Please forward your order to: Sonia Johnson, P.O. Box 10286A,
Albuquerque, NM 87184, (505) 344-4790